VERSE
AND
VISIONS:

Finding Grace

John T. Eber, Sr.
MANAGING EDITOR

A publication of

Eber & Wein Publishing

Pennsylvania

Verses and Visions: Finding Grace
Copyright © 2009 by Eber & Wein Publishing as a compilation.

Library of Congress
Cataloging in Publication Data

ISBN 978-1-60880-005-6

Proudly manufactured in the United States of America by

Eber & Wein Publishing
Pennsylvania

Foreword

As I read through many of your comments and personal statements, I couldn't help but notice one word that was regularly mentioned: Outlet. Where many of you indicated how poetry provides an outlet for creativity and honing in to improve one's writing ability, others claim it is an outlet to escape pain, sorrow, or everyday stressors. And even a small number confess how writing a poem is a personal cleansing process with nothing but a purely cathartic purpose. But whether indicative of a creative outlet or a therapeutic one, I found the imagination, motivation, passion, and raw emotion behind the verses in this collection truly remarkable. The nice thing about such an outlet is that it encourages repressed feelings and emotions to surface and even instigates new approaches to past events—for example, what once triggered painful, melancholy feelings might later welcome witty, lighthearted humor after a period of reflection. Or just the opposite may happen when experiencing tragic loss or the death of a loved one. Although poetry shouldn't always be limited to just personal experiences, such experiences shared in this volume are quite moving, and we are honored to publish them. I can't say how many times I've been told that poets draw a great deal of inspiration from reading other poets' work and how even a secondhand witness of their experiences can be powerful and influential. I hope this is the case for you and that you find all of the poems in this volume worthwhile. As a teacher, I always stressed to my students that there is nothing more refreshing, invigorating, or educational than for a poet to read another poet's work. Poetry is a craft to be shared and you have ultimately provided us and each other with small glimpses of the world as it exists through your eyes. Continue to be free and let go!

John Eber Sr.

The Necklace

A butterfly—
A blue one.
With gold
Around the edges.

It seems to
Flutter
And to fly.
It floats around my heart.

It is so simple,
Yet superb.
It is an exquisite
Heirloom necklace.

Rebekah Hovey
New Berlin, WI

My Mom

If they were rating Mothers,
My mom would rate a ten.
She stood by us all.
Through good times and bad,
She was the best Mother, Anyone could ever have.

She loved music,
Played her piano everyday;
Especially the hymns.
She made holidays extra special,
Baked all kinds of cookies,
And lots of cakes and pies.
We loved her holiday dinners,
She put much time and love into them.

She loved her home, and it showed,
Mr. clean helped her make that known.
She always listened to our troubles,
And gave us good advice.
She welcomed us home; with open arms.
She was a lady with great charm,
With love in her heart and music in her soul.
We miss her more each day.

Betty J. Roseberry
Baltimore, MD

Walking with Jesus

I followed Jesus one glorious day,
and this is what he had to say:
He said, "Someday you'll be man,
and I will lead you to the promise land.
Now here you are and your days aren't as long.
At the end of your journey, your days will be done.
Now they are so don't be afraid.
For you are walking with Jesus this very day."

Monty Leigh
Waterville, NY

About the Sea

Now I don't know what's bothering the sea,
so rough by the afternoon.
As usual the same one of Coney Island, the sure one from
yesterday and yes the one from this morning. When the
tides were in quietude, a sleep in a solitude mood.
Now as evening falls a suave clear blue sky and winds stirs the
tides, mouths are open and an echo, that echo that hammers the
shore, they come, away they send me of my spot.
Tides rise height, one after the other they run
Chasing the shore and I'm walking I take off. I take off.
But those white and blue silhouetted loot my departure...
I run, I move away and when I hope to be far there my heels
the kiss. And I smile, smiiiile.

Nelson A. Flores
Jamaica, NY

3

A Picture

Intrigued captured, not knowing who you are
but secretly enchanted by your look.
Only your picture I see place in my
photographic memory as I visualize what it
could feel like in the presents of you. A secret
imagination amazed, patiently I wait to hear
your voice with nervous energy but relax and
ready. It is a feeling I want to share a smile
deep within an enchantment of rides. " We
could dance in the rain hold each close in
the winter and flowers would never die
because of you". If I could touch you, I am sure
pleasures of joy would fill my heart that is
already calling out take me, pick me. A
mystery or puzzle, I am fascinated by your look
in a daze wondering if only the chance to hold
you not letting go is my dream. A history we
are building maybe a lifetime together, it is the
memory I will treasure right now today. I am
stimulated still holding on, embrace for
whispers that bring warm words with joy and
laughter. It is only your picture I see only a
picture.

John M. Groover
Roslyn, PA

I enlisted in the US Navy after graduationg from high school. While in the Navy I started
writing poetry or daily thoughts I would call them. After leaving the Navy, I started
working for the government and that's when I really began to write. I would write poems
for co-workers who would be leaving for a new position or retirement. My family, AJA,
Ivy, John Jr., Shanyah, Desirie, Brandon, Summer, Michale, Kaleem, Aynita, Tyrese and
mother Ms. Johnnie of course--I love them! The love of my life, Arlene, inspires me to
keep on writing and finishing my book.

Lover's Prayer

In truth

What is done
cannot be undone

Absolution

Not a paperweight
for passion's pain

Remorse

A penance
for not having seen

The inevitable

Yet of all
that is left
of who we are
and what we are

Our love

Can never be taken
from us

Nor ever the grief
of the unrequited...

S. R. Palumbo
East Meadow, NY

To Where Is My Mare?

Lavishly, a sunlit meadow sits agleam,
Its blades, wind-blown, beam,
Unto the skirting hillock's bosky stream.
Valorously, welkin abets the verdant ridge to glee,
Amorously, coalescing itself with the sea.
Musingly, a prowess steed roves the meadow free,
Fancying thus, a mare, doth it seem.

A flaxen windswept mane, flickers as fire's last fame,
Cascading to chestnut shoulders, as thickset as boulders.
Herculean hooves riving ground, as Zeus' bolts thunder doth sound.
A passion conveyed gaze, veiling wild eyes ablaze,
Seeking what he must, to quell desire's lust.
Lovelorn, doth the pace quicken, for he be, lasciviously stricken.

Alas, as the celestial skies falter,
Unto black night's occult altar,
Revealing dazzling diamond's desire,
To once again set the world afire,
Aurora conjures a morrow of mirth,
As Pan's eyes wield sorrow to such birth.
Akin, muses he to how he shall fare,
Living about the wide world, less a mare.

Christopher Ellwood
Columbus, OH

What You Are to Me

Have you any idea what you are to me?
Do you know how I feel? Do you know what I see?
A bright, growing girl with a warm, smiling face;
You were first in my heart, had the first special place.

You're part of a link, a piece of a chain.
You're funny, you're somber, you're fancy, you're plain.
With you, I feel daring to try different things.
With you, there's a magic like horses with wings.

A unit we make with three other folks,
Who tickle each other and tell corny jokes.
We travel together, learn words to a song,
Share bits of each other, the short and the long.

Have you any idea what you are to me?
You're the chips on my chocolate, the mint in my tea.
You make everything brighter, so now do you see
That the you and the I make the whole of the we?

Leslie Chasse
Willimantic, CT

Widow, Aftermath

In the beginning
After you died,
I sat, alone,
A solitary figure.
Object of sorrow.
Defined by despair.
Unmoving, unfeeling.
Lifeless, as a fly
on sticky paper.
Then, as days became weeks,
And weeks moved into months,
I slipped back into life,
Gradually, noiselessly.
Where once there were two,
Now an entrance of one.
I had choices to make,
To be a pea in a pod,
Unseen, unheard.
Or a flower in bloom,
Filled with all that is life.
I am that flower,
The journey continues.

Doris Guttman
Boynton Beach, FL

Death Is a Personal Thing

Every Death is a personal thing
Whether we go or stay
We pass through this journey
Each in our own way.

To some it comes quickly
To others long and slow
Some go quietly
Some are just suddenly gone.

Some surrounded by loved ones.
Some need that final moment alone
Some embrace it; some fight it all the way
But it comes, inevitably it comes,

And when they are gone from our life
We are sad, we hurt, we cry
Then like the sun coming out
We begin to remember

Not the big things especially
But the little things
The things they said, the things they did
The 101 silly little things that make them-them

They touched our life just by being in it
They add something to it
They are forever a part of us/our life
And we are never quite the same.

Kim Lewis
Independence, MO

Moving On

He stands, a hobo on the track,
devoid of the baggage of years,
lethargy cut into the line of his back,
a whistle the only sound he hears.

Around his jagged stick I tie
a kerchief sack of memories.
Heavy as stone, fling it high
beyond your boxcar frieze.

To the next stop, and the next, rumble along,
don't let a memory fall.
Carry them—with you they now belong—
To a station beyond recall.

But when all that's left to see
is a vanishing puff of black,
it's I who am aboard and he...
he stands, a hobo on the track.

Elaine F. Lindenblatt
Tappan, NY

We Are One

It seems like only yesterday
When a gentle voice did I hear say

Your pencil may I borrow please
His charm and smile seemed caressing me

With time and talk we merged tender, young hearts
Our love grew, impossible to part

A lifetime bond had now begun
Though some doubted, thought it was fun

Our love and devotion grew stronger with years
With each other standing strong against all fear

Forty years have since passed by
Like a dream, sweet, in a blink of an eye

Wonderful. Wonderful it would be to enjoy forty
more
If instead, it's meant to be, we'll meet again at
Heaven's door

How grateful we are to have enjoyed lifes gifts
For on angels wings our time was so swift

We are the lucky ones with family, friends and yes,
the fun
Together, Forever, we have always been one.

Joan Kowalski
New Richmond, OH

Untitled

We lost a soldier in September,
A young soldier we'll all remember.
His life cut short by an I.E.D.,
While fighting to keep our country free.

He gave his life for the U.S.A.
The whole country should have stopped to pray
When we heard the news that awful night-
Gone too soon from his family's sight.

At his funeral three rounds were shot,
That cold, somber day won't be forgot.
People lined the streets with flags in tow
Affected by this terrible blow.

At half-staff our flags were flown that day,
Because that's the American way.
When the hearse went by, some people cried
As our young hero took his last ride.

Kathy Silva
Harrison, MI

Happiness Is

Happiness is a walk in the park, a light in the dark
The pinging of rain on a window pane, on a warm summer night
The first new bud on that tiny rose bush
You almost lost in last winter's rush
That's what happiness is

Watching the snow fall in the bright moonlight
Sitting by the fire on a cold stormy night
The little kitten you nursed back to health
That rich Aunt—who needs her wealth
That's what happiness is

A mocking bird singing to the trees
Tellen everybody—who's you who's me
The little pup waiting for you to come home
With a lotta meat on a little bone
That's what happiness is

The warm sweet look on my Mama's face
The country road that has no haste
The new braches on the tree you planted
The new lease on life that God has granted
That's what happiness is
That's what happiness is.

Helen Lovett
Plumsteadville, PA

The Hand That Never Spoke

The hand that never spoke.
Oh, the hand that never spoke.

It never helped me do my homework.
It never helped me write.

It never really did anything.
Just sat there and mumbled.

The hand that never spoke.
Oh, the hand that never spoke.

It never helped me hold my books.
It didn't want to come to school.

It wanted to do everything.
But it wasn't right

Oh the question mark.
Oh the question mark.

"don't start!"
Said the left hand.

Alexa Marinakis
Canton, OH

Godspeed

This wintry morn I took an hour to celebrate my hair:
—its softness to my touch
—its shimmer in the light
—the way it compliments my features
and curls happily around my chin.

It warmed my head this cold, cold day and covered frosty ears.
It was willing to go up or down according to my whim:
—to hide beneath a hat?
—get all decked out with stuff?
—be permed? sprayed? colored?
cut? curled? braided?

This hair and I, we've stuck together
in every sort of weather!
But now, it's time to part (no pun intended).

The time has come, this is the night, the hair must go.
Just one more way for cancer to bare my heart!

Carol L. Friesen
Minneapolis, MN

Candle Light

If I could have a wish to be it is for more candle light for you and me.
Born of wax, born of wick, life begins with the flame of a match.
The glow pierces the darkness to bring forth light unto the void of the world.

It is warmth, wonder and mystery for the observing mind.
The candle light pierces my soul and asks me over again, "Do I really Know?".
Do I know what is to be, as life, as an unraveling mystery, proceeds.

The children dance and sign about as those special days join the embrace of the wind.
Times passes as the seasons of life are illuminated by the quivering flame.
As the light begins to fade, the eternal cry is for more candle light to yet stay another day.

It was so good and bright I do tell.
My soul ignited with the ephemeral flame, dancing life's visions about.
Candle light, O' where are you to be, once we meet in eternity?

Timothy Jakubiec
Stittville, NY

The Creation

Before the earth was formed,
God had a wonderful plan:
He would fill the world with good things
And over it all place man.

First He made the heaven—
His home up in the sky;
Then he moved the seas aside
and left a large space dry

The dry space He called earth
and covered it with trees,
with grass so green and flowers so sweet,
And he put fish in the seas.

He made animals of every kind,
And none of them were wild—
The lions, the tigers, the bears and all
Were gentle, meek and mild.

The sun was made to light the day
The moon to shine at night:
And every where you look you'll see—
"God's Creation" a glorious sight!

Ida M. Hall
Hyattsville, MD

First Day of Preschool

He stopped dead in his tracks
Crossed his arms and said
"I not your baby. Don't say that anymore."
"I a big boy now. My birthday made me 4."

"Oh please," I beg.
"No, no, no," he says.
"I big now, see"
And he stands up on tiptoes and…grins

"But, you're my youngest," I explain
"you'll always be my baby,"
"Even when I'm a hundred
And you are fifty-eight."

Then, we get to school
And he goes right in.
And I'm left standing there with tears.
'Goodbye little man," I say.

Kathy Freyberger
Dubois, IN

Only One Stood

I was on my way to Calvary,
  going to see the Lord.
When I saw a mighty battle
  of angels carrying swords.
It was good against evil,
  evil against good.
When the battle ended,
  only one stood.
I saw Archangel Michael,
  with his flaming sword.
Leading God's army,
  defending our Lord.
It was good against evil,
  evil against good.
When the battle ended,
  only one stood.
Upon the battlefield,
  I saw a dove descend.
The angels laid down their swords,
  the battle it did end.
It was good against evil,
  evil against good.
When the battle ended,
  only one stood.
The war seems never ending,
  each battle takes it's toll.
But I will take the side of Jesus,
  I want to save my soul.
Good overcame evil and
  evil succumbed to good.
"Prophecy fullfilled and only One stood."

Michael Ermolovich
Willow Grove, PA

21

In the Night

As I lay here in the middle of the night,
I long for your arms to hold me tight.
I can feel them though you're miles away,
how often I think of you night and day.

I can almost feel your body next to me,
Releasing this magic that needs to be free.
I call out your name too often I know,
begging and pleading please don't go.

But I realize it's just a dream,
things aren't really what they seem.
You aren't yet lying by my side,
These feelings just need to be pacified.

I can wait for you this I know,
as the seasons come, and the seasons go.
Because I feel deep in my heart,
We were meant to be from the very start.

Dotty Callahan
Farmington, NH

What Are Material Things?

People are always saying…material
things can always be replaced. But not
memories of past loves, and loved ones
that come and go with those material
things…yes some material things
hold painful reminders. But they
also hold cherished mementos of
loved ones no longer here to share
with…Memories of laughter , hugs,
and tears that you shared, all to
be torn away be estranged family
members. Even that of another evil at
noon or night, a storm that engulfs
everything from human life to home…
all memories washed away in a matter
of minutes. That took you a lifetime
to gather…so don't listen to those who
say that material things can be replaced…
it won't replace those items that
remind us of loved ones who
shared those mementos with you, or
the memories of laughter, sorrow
love and the jokes you shared with those
no longer here to share it with,
nor of the good times to come!

Letizia Davila
Austin, TX

The August Pool

The deep and serene August pool
One of the finest tools…of life
Along comes a person of Buddhist tendencies…
Caught in life's' abnormalities and strife.
He stops to close his eyes and linger there…
A meditations snare.
The creator's knife.
For the brief eternity he listens to nothing…
And that says it all…
To be suddenly startled…
By a wild-birds call.
Mind clutter begins to seep…
And the lovely waters fall towards the sea.
He rises and down the trail to another place he must be.

Bradley Collins
Sequim, WA

As the Snow Fell

Wandering a road
Lost in a snowstorm,
With nowhere to go but forward
No looking back
Because snow is all I see
But I remember
The way things used to be
Slowly slipping away
Like a shadow shrinking
At the crack of day
Yet never really goes away
Taunting you to try to fly
Away from where snow quietly
Falls from the dreary sky
Drowning you out
Including all cries
Of hopelessness you shout
But leaving you in a storm
Wandering hopelessly
In a dreamlike place
Where all you see
Is a chilling white
And you can't tell
The snowflakes apart
From the sky which they fell
Leaving you wandering lost
As snowflakes fly by
Hoping to see
That once blue sky

Anastasija Useva
Syracuse, NY

A Vital Relationship

We scream with our first

        We gasp with our last

   In between

We enhance you

        We destroy you

BUT ALWAYS WE NEED YOU

Gloria A. Almeida
Amherst, NY

Spring Will Come Again

Spring will come again.
The grass will grow green again.
The flowers will bloom again.
The trees will leaf out again.
The birds will build their nest again.
The birds will lay their eggs again.
The eggs will hatch again.
The birds will sing their songs again.
The Humming birds will be humming again
When spring comes again.

Darlene Powers
Dinuba, CA

Oversight Committee

Oversight is the act of an entity overseeing
to make sure that things are done right but somewhat confusing
there's another reason being:
in order to prevent oversight
know that oversight is synonymous with the word supervision
Yet ironically it also refers to an accidental omission
which is thenceforth regarded as mistake
While the foxes guarding the hen-house during this advantageous
condition indulge in the lion-shares take
Making convenient oversights after confidently acceding
appearing to honestly occupy the position of overseeing
with its two different faces though outwardly agreeing,
the one less than trustworthy with the one that's deceiving
So that the small-time investors are the ones left grieving
and if you think that's the end of all this shameless thieving
wise-up for your own damn sake
The bail-out plan has encouraged yet another brand of scheming
and you'll be ripe for the very next take
They will be slaking their greed as the economy is bleeding
therefore honest supervision is what we are desperately needing
that is free from the usual oversight
as is the case I'm now pleading
because with its opposing definitions
it's just grossly misleading

Chris J. Kuchenbrod
Brooklyn, NY

Love and Happiness

Love and happiness! Is there really such a thing?
Wish I could feel that warm and fuzzy feeling once again.
Really miss feeling that way.
I'm sorry that it couldn't stay.
Maybe I'll be lucky and it will come back.
Can't wait to feel warm and relax.
So until that time, I'll be patient and wait.
Just hope my love don't be too late.

Pearl M. Scott
Cincinnati, OH

Ship of Love

I feel as though I have missed the boat of happiness,
I'm stuck on shore while I watch others sail out to sea,
Why am I the chosen one, stuck all by myself why can't I flee,
I desperately seek for solace in heart that is full of despair,
Yet happiness strays from me as if it doesn't even care,
Sadness has consumed me taken over me like a plague,
Where did I go wrong for my life to be this way,
The light in the tunnel is dim, far from within my reach,
Perhaps with a little luck the benefits I can reap,
For a heart full of pain, empty with no sight of relief.

Bulent Isik
Carlsbad, CA

Words for Seniors

Years pass quickly like a sprinting jackrabbit.
Trying to slow them down becomes a daily habit
Never-ending dreams, filled or unfilled, become
life's biggest, hardest most desired necessity.
Many memories, brightening, saddening but never lost.
Humbling times, exhilarating times, always in mind.
Wishes, desires, regrets remain in our hearts.
Wanted, unwanted, loved or not loved.
Having children turns the spokes on the wheel of life,
lifting to great heights or dragging down to despair.
Children eagerly, busily, anxiously start a new life.
While seniors wearily, desperately cling to a diminishing life.
Fear, with its dreaded horns, is an evil part of living.
Frightening, lurking, worrisome, ever present, ready to pounce
on easy prey.
Grim determination, coupled with serious will and desire,
Help conquer the evil enemy, renewing our strength and survive.
Carefree laughter, smiles and music, become medicine for seniors.
Helping, caring, and loving are keys opening doors of happiness.
Though we cannot control the path of our destiny,
endless effort in the right direction can lighten our way.
Experiencing life to the fullest with faith, goodness and endurance,
helps seniors prepare for an unknown, unpredictable future.
Life is uncaptionable for in the end it disappears.
However, while it lasts, may it be ours to choose and enjoy.

Viola Massenzio
Milton, MA

Just Another Sunset

I rest on my friend's porch watching the sunset.
Grab an Amstel, put my feet up, begin to ponder and forget
About all the troubles in life, of past regrets and old memories
That lay to rest for the day. As does the sun over the distant trees.

Of future memories, too, which will hopefully come soon.
One never knows what to expect, only the coming of the stars and moon.
For she can one day come into your life with no warning at all,
And change it most suddenly, as if hitting a brick wall.

She would open me up and pick me apart.
She would study my mind and steal my heart.
By the end of it all she would know exactly what I am about.
With all of this occurring without me ever opening my mouth.

Too many questions, uncertainties that there would be,
But I'd be willing to give it a shot, hopefully so would she.
I cannot live for tomorrow, only for today.
Because such a chance might never, more than once, come my way.

So I continue sitting here watching the sun go back to where it came
from.
I've seen it all. Blue to Orange to Red to Pink—the entire spectrum.
How could something so simple make your thoughts so complex?
And how could His colors create so much beauty as they alter and mix?

I shake my head and realize it's not good to think so much.
Yet there were so many thoughts this day that upon I did not yet touch.
I take the final sip of my beer, put it down next to my chair.
I think I'll go inside the house now. I wonder if my friends are still there?

John Nycz
Lebanon, NJ

Old Gray

Once upon a time there was a wise old wolf
who'd not eaten a thing for days.
He suddenly spied a bull with one lame hoof
put out in a pasture to graze.
He leaped the fence and slunk forth to the kill
Which he did because it was pray.
He ate and he ate and he ate to his fill
then ran happily on his way.
With a leap, a prance, a howl of perfection,
He couldn't contain his feelings of joy.
All too soon he'd lost his sense of direction.
Like a snowball in the hands of a boy.
Two hunters while walking among the wood
Heard the cries Old Gray couldn't stifle.
Many times they'd done what little they could
to get Old Gray in the sights of a rifle.
They quickly sought shelter behind a large stone.
Soon the wolf would come into view.
He did, they shot him and he died with a moan,
Still in sight of the bull that he slew.
If you're wondering why this story is told;
why it was ever put to pen?
Never open your mouth when you're full of bull
is the moral that here lies within.

Jerome J. Tallent
Suncity Center, FL

There You Are

I look up on a clear night
and see a star twinkling in the sky.
I smile and think, "there you are."
I watch the sunset over the trees
and beyond the mountains.
The sky glows with shades of Orange and Pink.
I smile and think, "there you are."
A breeze sweeps across the earth.
And brushes against my skin.
I smile and think, "there you are."
A butterfly glides past me
and rests its delicate form on a flower.
I smile and think, "there you are."
A fallen leaf blows across the ground
And lands at my feet.
I smile and think, "there you are."
Snowflakes fall all around
and I catch one in my palm.
I smile and think, "there you are."
I feel my heart beating in my chest.
I smile and think, "there you are, always."

Travis Nuckles
Lynchburg, VA

Don't Tell Me What To Do

You were there,
With him that day,
I don't know why,
I say this:

You can't be,
At all near him,
You have to go,
The bell will ring,

I say "hey",
Hold up,
I can stay here all day,
So you can go,

Don't tell me,
What to do,
You don't know,
Who I am,

So I say,
Back off hot shot,
This is where I stand,
So find a new post,

I don't know you,
You don't know me,
This is where I am,
This is where I stand.

Leanne Conway
Millersville, MD

I Wonder If She Knew

I wonder if she knew when she awakened that morning
As the sun peered in her window and she stretched contentedly.
She wiggled her tiny shoes into her pale pink slippers
And walked slowly into the bathroom for her morning rituals.

I wonder if she knew when she poured her first cup of
french roast coffee. She carried it carefully to her favorite
aqua chair in the living room, flipped the remote control on to
the Today Show, enjoying Katie and Matt, as she did each
weekday morning.

I wonder if she knew when she showered and dressed for
the day. She wore lavender polyester slacks and a pink and
lavender shirt with her pink belt and sensible little white shoes.
She meticulously applied her Clinique make-up and favorite
fragrance, Estee Lauder's "Knowing".

I wonder if she knew when she walked proudly with her lucite
cane to the beauty salon in the rear of the building, where Lee
gently shampooed her silver hair and attractively styled it
and then she joined her lady friends for a light lunch in the
dining room.

I wonder if she knew when she won $6.00 playing Bingo that
afternoon, carefully placing those statistics in her journal.
She dressed slowly in the new navy and white pantsuit that I bought
her as she prepared to go to Prezzo's for dinner with Jack and Iris.

I wonder if she knew that she was living her last day on earth
and I wonder if she knows how much she is missed?

Joan Leader
Hollywood, FL

Jesus Cares

To see the pain on your face
But not know how you feel
My heart and soul only wishes
That somehow the break will heal

We are part of the Body of Christ
Our struggles we go through together
I will always be here beside you
But only God can make it better

It seems that time has stopped
As we look with our tear stained eyes
That no one knows the pain deep down
But Jesus always hears our silent cries

With his caring face and gentle hands
For what else can you possibly do
To be covered in His grace and mercy
As Jesus warmly whispers "I Love You"

Emily L. Moore
Greensboro, NC

Requesting the Honor of Your Presence

Standing at the vestibule.
Apple trees in spring white,
Bridal lace.

Cascading down the aisle.
Cobweb clouds flow by,
Underskirt silk.

Swishing past the pew.
Gracious breezes blow in,
Gossamer veil.

Kneeling at the altar.
Dark earth, waiting still,
Groom's velvet.

Exchanging love's vows.
Rain, whispering, floats down
Gold ring.

Stephanie Jenkins
Quicksburg, VA

Black Humor

Not Evil, but
misdirected Energy;
an animalistic Alpha Male,
the Leader of the Pack;
Hero of the Damned and Idol
of the Lost.

Overwhelming, pervasive sLaughter,
clarity of thought found
in absolute Dementia.

pulse-pounding Disturbia,
Alienation by love of flame.
Screaming tires, Exploding glass,
glorious Pain, Volcanic excitement.
The self-proclaimed

Agent of Chaos.

Kaitlyn Maloney
Washington, D.C.

The Trilogy of Two

You were there…A firefly in the forest;
   A desirable future us overshadowing the me that was imperfect,
While forecasting the us that was perfection.
       Change and growth through time
       Spelled the trilogy of two for me, you and us.
You were elusive…Exciting…Attainable.
       My porous net became indiscernible in the dark, exciting chase.
Caught! The firefly of you transcended into a brilliant fire of us;
More you…Less me.
       Change and growth through time
       Spelled the trilogy of two for me, you and us.
As the seasons passed, the firefly of us grew brighter;
   more so than any celestial body.
The light illuminated us, and slowly…As infinity changes from mass to
   energy, the flaws of my net became apparent.
       Change and growth through time
       Spelled the trilogy of two for me, you and us.
The flaws multiplied into gaping holes.
   The illuminesence began to wane until finally the rim alone
remained,
And as the net that held us vanished, so to the fire…
And there was only me!
       For time is change and change is life;
       Life is growth and growth is death:
       Change and growth through time,
       Spelled the trilogy of two for me, you and us.

Frank Williams
Hernando, FL

Epitaph

A common man spoke in a dream
That some might call a silly scheme
What can he say, that minds so great
Did not in past pontificate?

Yet in the book of life we write
And try our best to live it right
In thought, word and deed we pray
Too far from that we hope not stray

In youth misspent on worldly things
And wants that only money brings
Builds mansions on loose sand that fall
To crush those things bought at the mall

Seems only with advancing time
When skin and bone begin decline
That old eyes now with wisdom see
How fruitless was that search for me

Short is our life journey and the roads last bend
When age and shadow become your friend
Will you then also have a dream and find
Your own better words to leave behind?

Or might we deserve these simple words instead
Etched deep in stone above our head
That marks the spot where we now lie
"This day was born – This day did die
Each day between – live right – did try"

Edward Sobeck
Lemont, IL

Perception

In a world of color and light,
Darkness,
Hues of black and gray,
Is what I see.
I see not only the peace and happiness,
Your eyes trick you into seeing,
But the resentment and poverty,
Of our true world.

That is not all I see,
I see all that you think you see,
But under a dimmer light.
I see colors as you do,
But I understand what they truly mean,
Too.

They say that there is joy,
Hope compassion, truth,
But you only see that part,
I see the whole.
One without the other false.
Look through my eyes,
And then your own.

Chelsey Shindler
Woodbridge, VA

Smile

Smile a while
and while you smile,
there are miles
and miles of smiles.

Barbara Brackett
Forest Park, GA

Goodbye

Some say never
Some say for now

Few say okay
Few say O' rat A' tat tat

Little say nothing
Little say silence

The bold say forever
The old say see ya later

What do
You say

Vickie Johnson
Elbridge, NY

Small Town

I walked today just up the street,
and oh, what I did see.
Pretty flowers blooming everywhere,
and in the park a tall oak tree.

I passed mothers' pushing baby carts,
and old men sitting in the park.
Sunbathers were enjoying the warm sunny day,
and the park swings were filled with children at play.

I heard a train whistle in the distance,
and watched as the train gates came down.
The ice cream truck has stopped at the corner,
there is so much life in this old town.

At the far end of Main Street nestled in the trees,
is a quaint little tea house, they serve pastries and cheese.
I walked in and I ordered some raspberry tea,
I returned smiles with many that I was so glad to see.

I started walking back home feeling so refreshed,
the beauty of a small town makes one feel so blessed.
Just ahead is my house: the porch swing is moving in the breeze,
life is so good here, and I feel so at ease.

Wilma Clippinger
Carlisle, PA

Invitation to Lake Michigan

Capturing the beauty along the lake shore
A secure moment in surrender to nature
Refreshing air providing a restful breath
Colorful water soothing in motion and sound
The sun is shining with a warm brilliance
Water upon sandy shores so soft and cool
Majestic sand dunes created by wind and water
Tall swaying trees high above the dunes stand strong
Sounds of seagulls having a purpose are welcomed
Stones washed ashore are unique in color and shape
A wonderful awareness of uninterrupted pleasure
Boundless skies arching over the vast horizon
A sunset vivid in colors is a work of art
The day is giving way to night so gently
A full moon casting light with a company of stars
Glistening soft light reflects upon comforting water
Realizing contentment is just a stone's throw away
Whether it's winter, spring, summer, or fall upon the lake shore
What pleasure in knowing people and nature are content
A romance once again is inviting to Lake Michigan

Michael F. Cagney
Whitehall, MI

Ode To a Bowl of Truffle Soup

"Might you try our soup truffle?"
The waiter retorted;
'Twas a sly invitation
At a price unreported.

When you're out with friends dining,
An affluent group,
Would you 'ere think of asking
The price of a soup?

They trafficked in truffles;
They turned them to soup,
So with fervor unmuffled
We said "aye" in a group.

'Twas a flavor delightful,
Not a drop did we spill,
But our bill was most frightful,
And it made us all ill.

Truffles are black,
But we are all blue;
We trifled with truffles
And got quite a screw,

Over fungousy foodstuffs
With flavor exhalted
We ingested with savor
But got wallets assaulted!

Martin C. Mayer
Boynton Beach, FL

The ode was the result of a visit with friends to a NYC restaurant where all soups on the menu were within the $5. to $8. range. When we got our bill, truffle soup was billed out at $35. per bowl. I wrote the Ode so I wouldn't explode! Humorous verse is a cathartic palliate.

Christmas Poem

With joy and a lot of good cheer,
Christmas day once again is here.
Plenty of food and presents to share and
No one seems to have a care.
But something is missing on this wonderful day;
Did anyone remember to stop and pray?
Let's just look at what this day means,
It really is more that it seems.
Remember the birth of that little child?
Who came from heaven for such a short while,
If only people would stop and pause and think
That it's not all about Santa Clause.
Jesus' birth that happened so long ago.
We seem to forget our future He holds.
So as we celebrate this Christmas Day,
Let's all remember our Respect to pay.
To thank God that He sent His son,
A gift that can never be out done.
This year at Christmas, let's all take time
To keep Christ in Christmas, our Savior Divine.
So when the sun sets on this day,
Our joy will be found in the right way.

Madaline Hammond
E. Bridgewater, MA

I wrote this poem because of the way people were responding to what Christmas is all about. I was shopping and said, "Merry Christmas to the cashier who replied that he couldn't say Merry Christmas and had to say Happy Holidays". This thought went through my mind and kept me awake until 2:00 A.M. I arose and wrote this poem. People don't have to listen to what you say, but putting it in writing is always an option for them.

Jesus

I tried, Lord, ain't nothing else
for me to do, but trust in you.
I am through, I've done my best.
Jesus you can do the rest. I give you
my nest. I'll take it one day at a
time, I am through. Jesus I trust you.
I sometimes cry. I tried, Jesus please
stay at my side. I don't know what is
happening to me. Jesus you are all I
have left. I believe you are the best and
I don't need the rest, unless they pass
your test. Jesus only you know the best.

Shirley Mason
Baltimore, MD

Pictures

Do you ever pick up the photo album and reminisce about the past?
Your life is there before you just as long as pictures last.
The baby pictures, always cute, and those you want to hide.
The growing up, the weddings with new people by your side.
The aging makes pictures more precious as we re-live our passing years.
The fun, the joys, the changes, and the pictures that bring the tears.
But how nice to have this record of our lives right there in view.
To pass on to our children so they can reminisce too.

Ann B. Germaine
Springfield, VA

Dream Come True

Still not smiling, can't believe it's you
I lived to see the day that was to never
come true.

A part of his story that won't be swept
under a rug
or hidden like other secrets heard with a
tiny bug.

There were no screams of come one,
come all or hear ye, hear ye.
People of all shades knew they should be
walking the beat, going door to door
telling of the party where Barack is the
star.

As I walk up and down the block
everyone screams, Barack! Barack! Barack!

On November 4th 2008
our minds were in a happy state.

We helped at the poles to reach our goals.
Now that he's in, will we help our friend?

Don't stop here and think we're through
We still must help this dream come true.

Regina Robbins
Phildelphia, PA

47

Sweaty Laughter

Sweaty laughter
Head tilted back
The green of my eyes hold for an instant
The dim lustful light
Hanging in this dingy, daring room

I feel a swell of vigor
As my hips ache for your touch
I want you to crave me when I'm out of sight

Ask me to stay…
Please, for all my teasing
I really only longed to be held

And your arms look like the ones
I've been waiting for

When the night ends
And you've said nothing
Only intently studied me

I feel…
Like a hurt specimen
What is it about me that only beckons your eyes
Not that space on your chest so good for a weary girl's head.

So I fight my own battle with my front door lock
Keys jingle and fall
I curse
Home alone this night—again

Linda Quinn
Glenside, PA

Secondhand

My car is not new
And the couch it was given
By a friend who wanted
New for her "livin'!"

My house it was lived in
For eighty or so
And I moved here
Because I needed someplace to go.

My clothes are garage sale
And so are my shoes
Secondhand everything
Even the news.

Everything hand-me-down
Nothing brand new
You save lots of money
How "lucky are you"

I was sitting here thinking
A moment ago
There's no place to buy
A used casket, that's so!

So I'll just have to die.
That's what I must do.
In order to get
Something brand new.

Marjorie A. Smith
Salineville, OH

An Angel Hiding

Positioned before the ocean,
With the water covering your feet,
Slowly sinking in the sand
And sweating from the heat,

Watching the waves tumbling in,
You see flickers of luminous light,
Almost as angels are rolling toward land
After a long and weary flight.

You continue to gaze
At this marvelous scene
And begin counting these angels...
Realizing there's more than fifteen.

All along the shore,
They struck quicker than lightning
And as you witness this miracle,
Your belief begins heightening.

Wherever you go,
There is an angel watching you.
So, believe even when you can't see
Because this miracle is true.

Jeffrey M. Boyd
Abington, PA

Change

It appears easier to stay where we are.
Staying put even if it is in mud up to our knees.
There is dry fertile ground just a few steps away,
But, alas, the mud is so familiar.
You have been here so long.

To reach freedom, the new, requires movement.
Just taking the few steps to the dry fertile ground takes courage.
Find the spark within to create an image of change.
Allow the feeling from the image to build and grow until...
It inspires the first step.

Let the image and momentum carry you forward
Bit by bit, until...
At last, dry fertile ground!
The journey, now complete, can inspire others
As they can now see clearly the path you have created.

Megan Mast
Dublin, OH

If Only I Had Known

If only I had known the angels would beckon you home.
If only I had known.

I would have walked a little slower.
I would have held you a little closer.
I would have seen things a little brighter.
I would have hugged you a little tighter.
If only I had known.

I would have spoken a little sweeter.
I would have heard you a little clearer.
I would have prayed a little longer.
I would have loved you a little stronger.
If only I had known.

If only I had known the angels would beckon you home.
If only I had known.

Shelley Vargo
Pearland, TX

A True Friend

A true friend is always there,
To lend a helping hand
They are always there to listen,
And to simply understand.
Someone to tell your secrets to,
To always lend an ear,
So they can whisper theirs softly,
Right back for you to hear.
They are always sure to be there,
To give a loving heart,
To always hold your hand,
So you will never be apart.

Ally Magnin
Oconto Falls, WI

Voyage

Life. Dark. Alone. Lost. Drowning. Fleeting.
Isolation. Depression. Jaded. Walls. Black.
Falling. Pain. Slipping. Spinning. Persecution.
Death. Welcomed. Wanted. Separation. Reaching. Searching. Broken.
Pursuit. Vision. Hope. Trust. Rejection. Fading.
Experience. Truth. Moment. Confusion. Repentance.
Surrender. Altered. Acceptance. Death. Loosed.
Respond. Birth. Reborn. Mercy. Freedom. Grace. Inclination.
Wholeness. Joy. Altared. Peace. Salvation. Life.

Terri L. Jordan
Midland, VA

For Grandma

Searching in my heart for the right words to say
Understanding that life will turn so many different ways.
Heaven is the place you were meant to be
We are so happy to know that you are finally free.

Rid of pain, sorrow and fear
What we need to do now is hold each other close and near.
All the great things you shared with us to remember and keep,
These wonderful memories will help us while we weep.

You are so beautiful in ways you will not know
I think that's why it is so hard to let you go.
Wondering the day I'll be blessed and see you once more
Hoping it's not far, that's for sure.

Expressing the love you gave to me
Thank you, Grandma, for helping me see
The beautiful ways he wants us to live
Caring and sharing, not receiving, but to give.

You are the best a person can possibly be
Just as beautiful, like standing by the sea.
I'll look up for you deep into the sky
As a little tear falls from eye.

Love you so much, always and forever.
In my heart, we'll always be together.

Stephanie Grandy
Canal Fulton, OH

The Failing Light

At birth we were link to the earth untamed, unnamed,
unclaimed and unashamed of our nakedness.
Wearily waiting securely and assuredly in the womb with
the placenta and by the umbilical cord.
It was a warm secure world full of nourishment and
encouragement.
We snatched unceremoniously from that world.
Our lungs were near bursting for the new element called air.
We were slapped tenderly as a welcome to this new world
and we came blinking and crying to this new environment.
If we could articulate, we would have said, "what is the name
of all that's holy is this"?
Then we received our first kiss, from this new and wonderful
creature we soon learned is our birth mom.
Encouraged and assurance by that warm kiss and smile that
said "Welcome, Welcome".
I discovered a new muscle (smile) and new warmth that
would, if I could, walk a mile for.
For the longest time I was meeting new creatures all the same
but different. It was all-new but nebulous.
It was all new and I was a boy and suffered tears and discovered joy.
My growth was fast from this new nourishment and encouragement.
Joy o'Joy where are those days? At times I think I need the haze.
If I thought she could spare the room I wouldn't mind returning
to the womb.

Gena M. Mason
Kansas City, KS

My Brother

If you know someone who always talks
And always trips when he walks,
Then that is my brother Jake

If you know someone who's filled with joy,
But tends to cry when he loses a toy,
Then you know my brother Jake.

There is someone who is very funny and
Makes a rainy day feel sunny,
And that is my brother Jake.

I know he always does annoy,
But he's my brother,
He's our family's little boy.

He is Jake!

Sydney J. Miller
Glen Riddle, PA

Untitled

It's a dark, cloudy morning
But I am awake.

My body tells me to move slowly,
But I am awake.

There's much to do in the house
But I am here.

My mind lists all things awaiting me
and I am grateful

I am awake and here.

Julia G. Mullen
Culver City, CA

Starfish Stupor

Seductive shapely starfish stretched out on the hot sand
Luxuriating, toasty, ever so slightly tanned.
Sensuous sun rays caress them, a day relaxed, unplanned
Startling the starfish the sea begins to reprimand
Imploring, compellingly sparkling water speaks their demand
Spellbound starfish slither to the sea as if under its command.

Julie David
Reisterstown, MD

Living Love Lost

I've always walked to my own beat
    following my path as I watch my feet.
Then one day I risked a glance
    and I know seeing you was more than chance.

From the first moment our lips touched,
    through those times I felt my heart crushed,
in the words you never meant to say,
    there my beating heart shall stay.

Please always remember
    those months we spent together,
and know on this December
    that my heart's been yous forever.

I'll think of you every day
    as you slowly, slowly drift away.
Into life, out into the world,
    how can a loving heart feel so cold?

I need you here I need you now.
    I know I can love let me show you how.
But whoever you choose him or me,
    hold me always in your memory.

Jonathan Brusnahan
Chandler, AZ

I Don't Have to Fight

I don't have to fight anymore
For the love that I need
For my God is the one
Who will give to me
All that I will ever need

I don't have to fight anymore
For the happiness that I want
For God will give me
Rainbows and moonbeams
Sunshine and rolling streams
And
love never ending
In all my dreams

God is the true love of my life
He is my absolute best friend
Who will supply all I truly need
Right to the very end

Nancy Sullenberger
Jermyn, PA

Withered

You can tell if he's wise
By his thickness of skin,
And strength of his conscience
Raping within.

The layers of depth
Peel from his face,
And then unto me
Deliver my fate.

My paper at hand,
I scream out these lies,
But truth is my heart
And this my disguise.

Sheena McKenna
Carrolton, KY

For Daddy D

It was hard for me to watch you fade away so fast,
I kept my fears and worries all bottled up inside
Instead of facing reality, I chose to retreat internally and hide
But there's no hiding from God's plan and what will be,
Not being in control is a hard pill for me to swallow
I haven't come to terms with you not being here with me tomorrow
The coolest guy I ever knew, a good dad, you did the best you could do
Our relationship was honest and sincere, you always remained true
We were a lot alike in so many ways
I just wish we could've been together for many more days
The thought of you not being around to watch your grandchildren grow,
Makes me so incredibly sad in ways that you'll just never know
But I've been abundantly blessed to have you for twenty-six years,
So with that I suppose I can wipe away some of the tears
I know you were listening to my very last request,
That's why you held on just a bit longer before you took your last breath
You endearing sprit is with me for all my days on this earth
And it is that unwavering spirit that I have carried with me since birth
The last words I spoke to you were I love you and see ya later
The time has come for me to let you go and allow you to be part of
something
Much greater.

Porcha Evans
Westchester, CA

At the End of the Day

At the end of the day, it's just me
Sure, we had our drinks and laughs like we do most days
But you went your own way again
So I went mine
Knowing what I feel is not a passing phase

At the end of the day, it's the same
An empty wineglass is all that is left of you
I can hear the ocean's thunder
So vast, so strong
But the crashing waves don't soothe like they usually do

Maybe one day when the world starts turning my way
And Fate and irony don't seem so cruel
We can walk the beach together and find ourselves
You, not someone else's, and me, not so much the fool

At the end of the day, it's all dark
I sit in front of the TV thinking that's okay
I help myself to whiskey
And then to bed
To dream that it's you and me at the end of the day

Wayne Mahaffey
Baltimore, MD

The Dance

Rest and get well
Renew your strength
Hear the whispers of the angels
Feel the kiss of God
You are adored
You are inspired
You make a difference
You cultivate love
You are divine
Spread your wings
Sing
Enjoy
This is your dance
Do not be afraid

Debbie Damron
Tucson, AZ

Of a Life Gone By

Years have gone by and I still lie awake going down memory lane.
My heart aches so as tears roll down, no one will know the pain.
Where are those helping hands I ask, and the shoulder I leaned for
strength.
The best part of my life went along with you, the day you left to rest.

Life without you was not meant to be, for we wanted to grow old
together.
Should I console myself in the faith I believe that nothing lasts forever.
The special times will never return when we were all together.
The memories that you left behind will have to do forever.
These memories span the life we shared and builds a special bridge.
That I cross over when I am lonely and sad to find strength and peace of
mind.

When I was just a very young girl you asked me if I was ready
To help you sail the ship of life through calm or stormy seas
I nodded in agreement but little did I know that you would leave me
alone
To sail that ship to shore. I am getting so tired of sailing alone, as I often
get
Lost on the way. The map of our journey is torn apart and I can't put it
quite straight.

Life was rough, we trudged along but regrets were few and far. We
Were so proud of the life we built for our children to carry on. I wish
you were
Here to see the beautiful fruits that grow on that family tree. You
nourished it
With such loving care to enjoy it alone saddens me.

Srimathi Hathotuwegama
Tustin, CA

My Last Cry

I'm tired of crying. I'm tired of hurting.
I'm tired of feeling like I'm nothing but a burden.
I'm tried of holding myself back.
I'm tired of living bad.
I'm tired of my life consisting of me being sad.
I'm tired of not knowing. I'm tired of being caged.
I'm tired of walking around life in a daze.
   I'm almost to the point where I'm tired of trying
   But most of all, I'm tired of crying.

I'm tired of being taken for granted.
I'm tired of trusting the unworthy.
I'm tired of coming clean to those who are dirty.
I'm tired of being lied to.
I'm tired of playing tug-of-war with my soul.
I'm tired of the devil trying to take control.
I'm tired of being stereotyped. I'm tired of racism.
I'm tired of my people forcing bad hands being dealt them.
   I'm almost to the point where I'm tired of trying.
   But most of all, I'm tired of crying.

Rondrick Knighten
Lubbock, TX

A Sister's Gift

Let these tears be captured,
May they be chastised for harboring regret.
Though irrepressible their downfall isn't inevitable.
Encircling me, I am soon accompanied
by your spirit
Giving me strength as your whisper
comforts my soul

"You are a great brother
You have done well."
"The faults of humanity, you are not accountable for
because your intent is sincere and not half-hearted."
"My existence was a sacrifice,
that you many understand that love and family
should never be ostracized."

This maimed heart has succumbed
to sorrow
"It's not right, it just isn't fair."
Waves of malice and hatred
targets the almighty
questioning,
"Why?"

Marcus Gray
Amityville, NY

Land-Locked

Snug harbored am I now,
Surrounded by familiar possessions,
Held in habit
Patterned for the measured comfort of the home.
I watch my children play,
Unafraid of sudden summer squalls or winter's rage
That engage other ports.
Content, they stay within the confines of the walls
Made strong by love and care,
Unaware of alien sight and sound.

Here is my life and here will I remain,
Secure and safe and ------bound.

Yet, rather I would be
On some harsh sea with you,
Straining for the shore,
Fighting the tide, the waves, the darkling sky,
Braving the fury of the hurricane
To find the "eye".
Daring to chart the strange and unknown course
Would challenge all my strength and wit
And courage------,
Ah, but it could be a wond'rous task!

To be together in the fragile craft
Is all I ask.

Jean Petranoff
Indianapolis, IN

The Rickety Bus

The rickety bus is hitting every bump.
Thank God it is not stumps.
The noise everyone talking at once.
The motor roaring loud.
Hope we get to Camp Hunt before the cloud.
The writing on the bus is a strain.
These bumps are a pain.
Camp Hunt here we come children and women.
I'll be there soon to get tea with lemon.
Horses, swimming, boats, fishing, and hayrides.
All kinds of fun and campfires besides.
Children frog hunting at night.
Women walking around with a flashlight.
Woods and trees galore.
Insects that make big sores.
Peace and quiet from the city.
The flowers so very pretty.
Church, prayers and Bible to learn.
All this fellowship in one.
For us someday to be with the son.

Margie Fishburn Rains
Indianapolis, IN

B4U

B4U I was fine alone, now, I'm not. I miss you when we're apart.
I was able to be lackadaisical not having to have to care.
>I was fine alone, now, I'm not. You're on my mind. I miss you.

I was able to sit in my chair, to calm my mind, sooth my nerves.
>I was fine alone, now, I'm not. I need your touch I love so
>much. I miss you.

I was able to cruse…get in my car & go, listening to my radio.
>I was fine alone, now, I'm not. I sing to you when we're apart. I
>miss you.

I was able to sit by the fire under the Oak, stare at the stars, watch the
moon hide behind the clouds…enjoy the night air. "I love the smell of an
open fire. Don't you?"
Oh, I forgot…
>I was fine alone, now, I'm not. I wish you were here & you're
>not. I miss you.

We're apart. Don't you care I'm not there, you're not here? I have my
doubts. I know you're a busy man. I keep telling myself I understand.
We both have things to do.
I come to you in the night; I leave you in the morning light. When we're
together without a word spoken, you express to me how you feel. What
we have is real! I have no doubts.
But, as I lay my head on my pillow & go to bed, I reach out—
You're not here. I'm not there. I'll dream instead.
B4U I was fine alone, now, I'm not. I miss you when we are apart.

Arlene Janovic
Glendale Heights, IL

71

The Rainfall Persona

A roaring hush
The rush of drops and splatters
Clatter the window with a tease
Endless ease down glistening grass—
all masked
By curtains, by tasks, by noises,
Poisons of the modern means;
Quarantine your indulgences a while—
Walk a mile with me, in me; wish-wish-wishing
Listen.
Listen to me.

Jamie L. Ogles
Scottsville, KY

Reflections

Subtle as a wind chime announcing its
presence by a soft twinkle,
Profound as a proverb uniting obscurity
with truth,
Empirical as applied to the philosopher,
with gentle humor as transparent as a
moonstone, yet capable of anger as that
breeze which slowly stirs a tai-fung.
Adieu, good friend...
The bird of time has but a little way to
flutter,
And the bird is on the wing.

Dolores Roney
Newhall, CA

Fall and Winter

Every season has such beauty!
Like the colors in the fall
That speak such wonder to me!
Autumn leaves and pumpkins bright
Are such a warm uplifting sight.
I sip a cup of cocoa and daydream in the night.
Savoring scented candles burning in a holder,
I ponder happy thoughts until
The wick begins to smolder.
The chill in the air makes us aware
That the holidays are coming.
The sights and sounds and decorations
And music keep me humming.
Then I look for snow and even though
To others it has no appeal,
I step out on the awesome frozen sea of fluff
And find myself enjoying how it feels.
Huge flakes of white whirling all around me,
Walking in a windy, winter flurry,
I smile and greet each one I meet,
It's too much fun to hurry!

Lucille Musto
Valley Stream, NY

I am a mother of five grown children, almost all of whom are out on their own. This leaves me with time to explore creative outlets. I like to paint, but recently I've been inspired to try writing poetry. Nature is a huge influence and inspiration to my pieces.

My Favorite Place

My favorite place is my backyard...
I see colorful birds chirping a wonderful tune
I see my pool it looks like a lagoon
I see a sky of light blue
I see orange marigolds too
I sit on bricks of red and gray
I wait for a sunrise that will start a new day
As I play with my soccer ball
The wind hits me and it feels like its Fall
I look down and guess what I see...
I see a four leaf clover that's just for me
As I hold my four leaf clover I look at a tree
With leaves all over in groups of three
I look at my green slide
I jump up and down and start to glide
Oops! I trip and fall
I don't get hurt but I hit my head on the soccer ball
I won't try that again too soon...
Or at least until I see the winter moon
A tree shaped like a cone is just what I see
A tree shaped like a cone is unique...just like you and me
My backyard is my favorite place, can you guess why?

Tori DiCicco
Massapequa Park, NY

74

The Ultimate Goal

One might consider the ultimate goal as being a billionaire entrepreneur such as
Bill Gates, the best known inventor of the personal computer and such,
Or Coco Chanel, a styling icon who designed clothes to dress women, a fashion buff.
One might consider the ultimate goal to be upholding the most powerful positions in the USA like
Barack Obama, making history becoming the first president as an African American,
Hillary Clinton almost becoming the first president of the United States as a woman,
Or Sara Palin, almost becoming the first vice president as a woman republican.
One might consider the ultimate goal to be a government official such as a policeman or fireman,
Saving and protecting lives as well as enforcing the law from people committing criminal sin,
And/or being a member of the Armed Forces, pledging their lives for their fellow countrymen.
One might consider the ultimate goal to be obtaining an important position in life such as
Becoming a famous person, great athlete or a big time celebrity,
Upholding a prestigious, important job such as a doctor, lawyer, or Indian chief,
Or, being a city employee, constantly keeping our community and environment safe and clean.

Ann Parker
Montgomery, AL

Fear—I thought

I felt fear when you said I love you.
I thought maybe the love would last or would it diminish.
I felt fear when you said trust me.
I thought on what grounds do you base trust.
I felt fear when you said believe in us.
I thought can I believe in you.
I felt fear when you said don't worry.
I thought what should I worry about.
I felt fear when you said we will be together for all eternity.
I thought it was funny but no one lives to see eternity.
I felt fear when you said I promise.
I thought what are you kidding.
I felt fear when you said I will never leave you.
I thought who is she.
You left—I felt no fear.
I thought nothing.

Jennifer Rixford
Scranton, PA

The Nature of Love

You are the beauty of the rising sun.
Cool colors followed by warmth and a moment that
takes my breath away.
Your blue eyes are the sky reflecting off the shimmering water.
So deep they go on forever.
Your skin is the warm sand beneath my fingers.
Always surrounding and comforting me.
Your voice is the whispering wind.
All around me, filling my ears with your perfect
sound.
Your love is a wave crashing then rolling on to shore.
Frightening and smooth all at once.
Sneaking up on me like a pleasant surprise.
You are the beauty of the setting sun.
Warmth followed by cool colors and a moment that takes my
breath away.

Lisa Whitman
Oceanside, CA

The New Deal

In 2008 there was an election,
that changed a country and inspired a nation.
It broke away from its segregated past,
And elected a president who was black, at last.

When Martin stood before millions and spoke of his dream,
America was not ready for what he had seen.
Because that time in history we were marching to vote,
Some considered his dream as merely a joke.

Martin would be elated if he passed this way,
to see what has transpired in his country today.
Throughout the years through history and time,
America has grown and expanded its mind.

We no longer use race as the ultimate test,
to find out who's better or who is the best.
It was not his color nor how he could speak,
it was his vision for America that made him unique.

No one would imagine with a name like he,
Obama could rise to the win the presidency.
Now that the election is over and won,
America's true test has just begun.

Now we must put our conflicts aside,
and build a nation of character and pride.
We now have been given the opportunity,
to show to ourselves how great we can be!

Carven L. Dukes
Beaumont, TX

What Can I Do to Better My Feelings?

My heart pounds and beats with sorrow.
My mind wonders about thoughts of tomorrow.
What can I do to better my feelings, and why do I feel this
way?

I regret plenty but still think about many.
The lives that were lost for no reason, so help me come to
conclusion.
What can I do to better my feelings, and why do I feel this
way?

Life is full of laughs then cries.
Living every day one step at a time.
What can I do to better my feelings, and why do I feel this
way?

Dad gone; Mom leaves; I'm bent down to my knees,
Saying God why but please help me figure out.
What can I do to better my feelings, and why do I feel this
way?

llorr Robinson
Stone Mountain, GA

A Better World

As we walk through this life...
We see the sadness, fear and strife.

But, if we only see that which is bad...
We'll never see the things that make us glad.

Beauty can be seen at every turn...
In nature, in people, we can learn...

To always see good in those we meet...
And find things around us that are sweet.

We should be positive examples to all when we can...
So we will make our world a better place for all man.

Linda Palatka
Owosso, MI

Where Do We Go

Here, here that time of year, school out parents take time off
Where do we go, where do we go
The beach, the mountains, the lake, let's go
Where do we go, where do we go
California, Texas, Florida, NH, Colorado
Where do we go, where do we go
A cabin, a tent, a hotel, or a trailer
Where do we go, where do we go
Rainy, cold, hot, or dry
Where do we go, where do we go
Super 8, Holiday Inn, Ramada Inn
Where do we go, where do we go
Room service, continental breakfast, restaurant on the corner
Where do we go, where do we go
Grandmother, Auntie Ruth, Cousin Beth
Where do we go, where do we go
Choose, pick, make up our minds
Where do we go, where do we go
Make a list, dog & cat to the kennel
Mail picked up by neighbor
Sister coming by to check house, water plants
Here we go, here we go
Door bell rings and a man in uniform is there
To say our son was killed in the Iraq war
What do we do, what do we do
We cry, we shout, we wonder why
Where do we go, where do we go
To the cemetery to say goodbye
That's where we go, that's where we go

Richard Pearson
Quincy, MA

What Is It About

I saw an invitation
In Soap Opera Digest
For all to enter
The Open Amateur Poetry Contest
It said I must hurry
So I wouldn't be late
The deadline for entering my poem
Is December 30, 2008.
Well my poem is original
It's 24 lines or less
What it's about I don't know
I'll just send it in and let you guess.
It might make you laugh you may even cry
But whatever emotion you experience
No doubt you'll heave a deep sigh
When you look at the other judges
As you toss it aside
You'll probably say
Well at least she tried.

Jean Hayes
Charleston, WV

I was born on Sept. 22, 1923, in Sewickley, PA. I was told my grandfather Hayes wrote poetry as a hobby, but I never knew him. My family was ordinary, musical fun-loving people. We loved to joke and make people laugh. Although I was born in PA, we lived all over WV. I started school in Williamson, WV, and later moved to Huntington, WV in 1935; I went to junior high there. We moved to Clarksburg, WV, in 1939 where I completed my high school education on June 1, 1941. When war began, my dad got a job at the defense plant in Charleston, WV. I went to work at Western Union Telegraph Co. on Aug. 5, 1942 and worked there until I retired on January 31, 1983 with 41 years service. Nothing in my life inspired me much to write a poem. I was so excited to learn I'd made it to the semi-finals. Just goes to show you never know what it's about until you try.

The Wind

I've never seen the wind, yet I know it's true.
As it whistles through the trees, I've seen what it can do.

At times the wind is gentle and whispers through the air.
At times it is tornadic and gives us cause to care.

I saw the wind blow off a hat. The hat blew down the street.
I saw the wind make ripples in a pond and that was really neat.

I've even seen the wind so strong, it toppled down a tree.
I couldn't see it with my eyes, no, the wind I could not see.

But though I could not see the wind, I'm sure you will agree.
The wind is real, it does exist, it touches you and me.

So even though I can't see God, by faith I know He's real.
He controls the wind I can not see, but it's results I feel.

Yes, God is real, He does exist for in my heart I know.
By faith I do believe in Him, my heart has told me so!

Marilyn Henning
Port Orange, FL

Winter at Ground Zero

The cold air blows through the trees,
The emptiness echoes, the pain lingers,
But with every frigid breeze the hope
Laces the frost with the warmth of peace.

Donna Kobel
Elmont, NY

Grades

Grades aren't like a potato chip,
They're like a game of battleship
It's only a game of strategy
It's hard for you, but not for me
Grades come after your test
Your only hope is to do your best
Grades go on your report card
You know you have to study hard
Try to get A's; they're the best
Do not worry about the rest
In Mathematics, Science, and ELA
Work extremely hard every day
In the end, it all comes through
The best grades, all for you
Summer vacation ends it all
No more grades until next fall

Warkah Scott
Brooklyn, NY

A Mother's Prayer

Bless this child, I've rocked to sleep
Make him strong and guide his feet
In righteous paths may he always tread
On scripture verse let his soul be fed
But if by chance my son should stray
Make him aware that every breaking day
She kneels at her bedside to pray and plead
To watch over her son and return him with speed
For she knows the pitfalls of Satan's snares
Heartaches that come when he thinks no one cares
Whatever the trouble, bring him home safe and sound
Let him remember by love, our family is bound
Christ has paid for our sins if we just repent
If we learn from mistakes, our time was well spent
Hear a mother's prayer, and send strength from above
Guide my son home to his family's love

Tandra Harper
Deep Run, NC

My Mother

My mom, so sweet, so beautiful, so bright,
A loving face—whose beauty won't run out.
She looks like the shiny moon in the night,
And is a person whom I think about.

She's like an angel flying in the sky—
So innocent, gentle, loving and right.
To her I go when I want to cry
Because she makes problems die overnight.

Her job is never easy—it is hard.
She teaches me to grow up to be strong.
I think of her being my bodyguard
Because she's there whenever things go wrong.

I love her from the bottom of my heart,
Because she stood next to me from the start.

Dana Awwad
Chandler, AZ

Imps

As you enter through these doors,
And walk upon these hollowed floors,
You may choose to spend the night
And hear a noise that gives you fright

Don't be afraid. Don't be alarmed.
I've lived here years, and still unharmed,
I've sought my life to catch a sight
Of those who scamper through the night.

I hear scratching on my walls.
Ghostly footsteps down the halls.
Heavy thumps above my head
That make me cower in my bed.

I hear them shuffle past my door.
With whispers, scrapes, and taps and more.
And tried my best to see if I
Could catch one glimpse with wary eye.

I hear them giggle at my side.
But, still, no matter how I've tried,
I could not catch one sight of those
Who interrupted my repose.

Until today, to my surprise,
I saw them smile from children's eyes.
These imps that scurry through the night;
They hide, in daylight, in plain sight.

Lee Beckstrand
Escondido, CA

Our Pastor

A woman of God to us was sent,
A woman of God on whom we can depend.
Sent from our Savior above with care,
One we can call on and know she's there.
Truly believing God's precious word,
Broadcasting his goodness to one and to all.

A woman we can call any hour of the day,
Know in our hearts Pastor's on her way.
Sent from our Savior above to be here,
To guide us and lead us without any fear.
Preaching his word just like he told her to do,
Praying and believing it will dwell in you.

A woman whose preaching comes from the heart with a glow,
Touching our soul as the anointing flow.
Lifting us up as we sing and shout,
Truly she's anointed and there's no doubt.
After all that she has taught us and all that we know,
How in the world can we let God go?

A woman whose footsteps anyone should follow,
Thinking today of a brighter tomorrow.
Seeking our Savior who's above,
Praising and thanking him for our Pastor we love.
Pastor preaching and teaching should abide in our soul,
Since Heaven has got to be our ultimate goal.

Halleluiah we'll say, she's the greatest Pastor sent from the Master.

Lauris Brown
Cincinnati, OH

My name is Lauris Brown. I am happily married (Joseph) with three children. Pete, Derek, Joyneida, daughter-in-law (Julie), grandson (DeSean). I reside in Cincinnati, OH. Fifteen years ago I gave my life to Jesus Christ. I'm save, sanctify and Holy Ghost fill. I do love the Lord! I attend the house of prayer under the pastoral leadership of Pastor, Doc, Deborah A. Lampkin. An anointed woman of God. I was inspired by God to write this poem because of my love for her. Also to write poems and songs for the writing to reach ministry.

The Lost Child

I miss you in the backyard,
with the green grass and the trees;

I miss your help around the house;
you were always sure to please;

I miss you in the car, when we would
go for a little ride;
You always watched out for potholes
you were such a perfect guide;

Is it true what the priests say,
you surround us in the air?

It must be so, because somehow we know,
that you still really care.

Elaine Gilmore
Westbury, NY

My America

Oh, how beautiful are you, my America,
Rolling hills that cover the Earth,
Mighty mountains that watch over
Her brothers and sisters, the plains and the valleys!

Green forests of trees that stand so erect,
Like soldiers defending our land!
Hail to you, America,
So beautiful are you!

We thank you for your beauty and peace,
Oceans that hover over us east and west
Rivers flowing throughout our land,
How beautiful you are!

America, my land, my home
I look at you with awe and sigh!
Gazing upon you, I am at peace,
Where my spirit can run free!

Joseph Giorgio
Manorville, NY

Untitled

You took me in
as one of your own
sorrow and pain I have known
safe in the shelter of your wings
I'm grateful for the love you bring
though I'm not of flesh and blood
my love for you is a flowering bud
Now don't you ever, ever doubt
my love for you shall never run out
with love so pure as the sky is blue
This love I have will always be true.

Luanna Studer
Hainsville, IL

This poem was written for my stepmother. When my father first introduced her to my siblings and myself, I would have nothing to do with her. I was very rude in fact. I soon was in need of help, and my father talked things over with Cathy and to my surprise they told me to move down to Illinios and live with them. She not only opened her new home to me, but she opened her heart as well. We became close and still are to this very day. I love and cherish her very much.

Season Within Season

As though it were reunion with a
Love estranged for months;
Embellished so grand in anticipation
Reality pales to it at once.

'Twas this how mistress winter
Settled in her long sojourn;
More irksome than I remembered her,
I picked up summer's urn

Of memories,
Swooning hopeful when I saw—
A likeness of her apple blossoms
Amid the rivulets of a thaw.

Romanticizing her nectar sighs, Mysterious
Lusts of eves immune mar—
And forgetting the oppression of her embrace
I swished inundate with nostalgia.

The day came when she unpacked her case,
Turned the sun up and fragranced the air,
And still ingratitude took hold of me,
For reminiscences had impaired

Her forthcoming, the same mirage
Dancing ahead of man's sands;
For summer is best when winter is in it;
Reading summer's letters under winter's command.

Nicholas D'olimpio
Worchester, MA

Autumn Is an Artist

As the windy cold air brushed against children's faces,
the orange and red tree leaves began to twirl down off the trees.
The weather became more brisk and the scarlet colors would fade.
Every day was so creative with bright tangerine and dark coffee colors.
Walking down the streets you would hear the crackling of leaves and the
crunch of children's footsteps, sounds you haven't heard in a while.
It was like a beautiful painting that came alive. Every day was
enlightening and elegant.
Whenever people look back they see it as the halcyon days.
The artist seemed so exotic but the artist itself is the great season Fall.

Kimberly Fedalen
Norwood, PA

Hi, I'm Kimberly Fedalen. I'm 13 years old from Norwood, PA. I am very honored
for my poem to have made it this far. Some thoughts that ran through my mind while I
was writing this poem were that all people should get to show their talents. The reason
that I wrote the things I did was because I believe that even the smallest things should
be noticed like fall. Those thoughts inspired me to write this poem and send it into this
contest. I'm glad that I did send it in because I believe that everyone should follow their
heart.

In the End

In the end I'd like to see
Jesus waiting there for me.
I'd like to hold his hand
As he takes me to the Promise Land.
I know that the ones who have
gone before me will be holding out
their arms to greet me.
I'd like to know my eternal home
Means that I would never be alone.
I'd like to be able to comfort
My loved ones and let them know
I will be there for them no matter
how long they have to go.
I would like my friends to know
it is okay to let me go.
Because no matter what I will
be there in the end.

Lynnette Keeney
Valley Head, AL

The Depression

I see my great Aunt Nini
laying in her bed
she is talking to me
she is shaking
the feeling is sad
she can't finish her sentences
she is depressed
I'm with no one but me
I see her with her cold skin
and white curly hair
she looks at me
then I leave
the sadness hurts
I miss her
the next morning I get a call
she's gone
I miss her pasta
I miss her kindness
I miss it all

Ashley Camarlinghi
Volcano, CA

Walk, Walk, Walk

And the final chapter of your life story comes to a sad and parting end.
The pages of your soul come to conclusion with that one last breath
That one last bid of farewell
It is not the ending, yet the beginning as the gates of heaven open
slowly...slowly
The Lord, Our precious Savior beckons you with open arms
Come Home, my son, Come Home
To a rest, full, Forever of Comfort
And as you close your worn and tired eyes in a slumber
A quiet moment
A Silence
Just a whisper of the symphony orchestra of the hall of angels
I see your face light up with joy
Home, Thank you, Lord, I'm coming home
I heard you spiritually call my name
And as I walk away in prayer, in a song
In a hour of celebration
I walk looking back for the last time
I see you wave Good-bye
To all the family and friends
It's gonna be all right
Home, Home...I'm going home
To my place of scripture
Where the weary and tired find rest forever in spiritual comfort.

Levonier Aldridge
Dudley, NC

The Apple of Life

When I was young,
I wish I could be an apple on a tree.
So shiny bright and freshly sweet,
The perfectness that life should be.
But that was only on a tree . . .
And we can't save all the trees.

Patricia A. Thomas
Port Matilda, PA

Prism Escape

I am the brilliance that dazzles the eye
When light rays are stopped.
And I don't let them by.
A bender and sorter of those who pass through
Ultra violet to red, through yellow, green and blue.
I am a diamond for those who pretend, a fortune of
Wonder in a small child's hand.
Expanding of galaxies, science has said,
Is shown by their color shifting to red.
In this I have been a useful tool, except there are
Some that are shifting to blue.
Likened to Doppler for measuring sound,
The universe is a merry-go-round.

William M. Price
Mystic, CT

Twilight

It is twilight and dovetail stars
are singing their final lullaby
of cream colored notes.

Sister Seyote sits with cobweb dew fairies...
they sip pineapple cocktails
in the fading mandarin sun.

The Popsicle children with their
grape juice lips and strawberry cheeks,
rise up and join hands...
they dance the dance of the moon keeper
and summon the Silver Lady
to her perch in angel swept clouds.

Tortoiseshell eyes, a string of abalone chips
'round her neck, a sharpened dagger
on her cocoa butter thigh—
she is the Huntress, waiting
for the creatures of still night to appear.

Cherry sorbet sky and sapphire stars
guide the way to the last Pegasus so that we might
Live in yellow sunflower days once more.

Andrea M. Jablonski
San Dimas, CA

Opening

O' dogwood flowers of purest white
you blossom even though the blight
of bloody cross and nails tinge red
thy white
And yet you bloom
as if to say rue not that day in pain
when you were crucified
but blossom
bloom now
today
Opening in purest love your rose seared snowy petals
O' open to the light
finding within thy center
a crown green and growing
O' open to the Light
Thou dogwood blossoms of radiant white

Bonnie Kendrick
Annandale, VA

Passion and Love

Virgin hands scared to touch,
But push on to discover.
Molding his lips to hers,
While tongues do a celestial dance.
Where coherent thoughts cease to exist
In the embrace of each other.
Passionate and patient to honor one another's flaming desires,
He looks down to smile at her.
The look on her face forever planted in his memories,
Her smile melting his manly ego,
Causing him to take a deep, satisfying breath.
The smell of tropical flowers swarms around
While his hand embraces her head for a more meaningful kiss.
A kiss deep, passionate, and yearning for more,
His hand traces down her spine and stops at the small of her back,
Causing her to come closer to him, to be one with him.
Smoothly he rubs the golden band around her finger
And whispers, "I will always love you."
Hand in hand in matrimony,
Showing what love really is.

Latashia Watkins
Conehatta, MS

Something That Rhymes with Six

Out of sight, out of mind
Out of line, out of time
Over here, over there
I'm gone, you're everywhere
Life is short, time is fast
Take control, make it last
Whoops, oh no, there it goes,
Out the door, on the road
Run run run, maybe catch
If you throw, then I'll fetch
I don't know what to do
If you go, I'll go too
Somewhere that we can hide
Look around, look outside
I will bend, you will break
It's my life, yours to take.

Caitlin Parmelee
Storrs, CT

Teacher's Rap

Please let me tell you what it's like with you
Every Monday through Friday brings challenges new
So to get your attention I will sing and tap dance
And try to deftly deal with each circumstance
You guys make it difficult, easy it's not
So I'm always looking for that sunny spot
To get you to grow in the ways that you need
I fertilize and water after planting each seed.
You're stars in the sky in the black of night
Positioned and poised with variances of light
The astronomer I am, bringing you into view
To find your place on the map to make your debut
I'm the lure, colored, sparkly and bright
Trying to get you to look, taste, and then bite
Reeling you in, with your complacency disturbed
We'll travel great places through numbers and words
I'm always the keeper and you're always the zoo
All strutting your stuff for each other to view
Ever the feeder and shoveler of dung
The critique of my job by the public I'm stung
If I do my job right my spirit I will renew
Some days you'll be the captain, some days the crew
I'll listen and remind you of your dignity and worth
And teach you to contribute to your home called Earth.

Rebecca Keese
Charlottesville, VA

Be Afraid

Be not afraid of who I am,
I'll help you out of any jam
talk is cheap and friends are few,
But for a price, I'll stick to you.
No need to look or search too far,
I'm right here at your nearest bar.
Just take a seat and sit right down,
I'll make you smile so you won't frown.
To heck with life—let's take a ride
who cares about your silly pride.
Let's drink to this or even that,
It's time for us to have a chat.
You're not the first to feel alone
To make excuses as you phone—
I've heard them all and that's no lie.
They say "come home" as they sob & cry.
Can't you have a drink or two?...
Without the guilt that sticks like glue!
I'm all you need to feel alive,
Now let's go and take a drive!
Who says you're drunk and cannot see
I'm right here, to set you free!
Well, my friend, it's time to go,
You're on your own, as you now know.
For you took a life so unaware—
Driving drunk without a care.
Time's run out; the price was high,
The name is death, that's who am I.

Elsie Cisneros
Oceanside, CA

Water Drop

Little water drop on my window pane
You're my only friend today
Don't go away for I love you so
Do you really have to go?

Maryann Gazdzik
Scottsdale, AZ

Regret

Regret is a lousy thing to live with
that is a fact of life and not a myth.

if you knew today was your last
would you spend it regretting your past?

Would you call your loved ones on the phone
Tell them you were blessed to have them to lean on?

Never put off till tomorrow what you can do today
Say the important things you need to say.

Don't waste your life holding a grudge
Leave it up to God to be the judge.

Velma L. Karr
Artesia, NM

The Old House

I wonder what stories that old house could tell,
The one resting there on the hill.
Mayhap would recall the time was new,
And each day was a sweet new thrill.

What joys it had felt at every new dawn
Amid the flurries of tasks to be done.
Then the feeling of peace at the end of each day
With challenges met and won.

It may tell of the love enclosed in those walls
The delight it brought whose within.
Then the thrill it felt as years passed bye,
As it saw each new life begin.

It could remember the times when tears crept in
And the light of joy would grow dim.
But faith was strong in the heart of that house
As it remembered all that had been.

The story might slow then as years passed by,
It would know it was time to rest.
The light in the window no more would glow,
But the house had given its best.

Ida Fortna
Pontiac, IL

Angels

Angels are everywhere in this mortal land
From the highest mountains to the beach's sand.
It may have been a husband or a loving wife
Or a close friend that has passed through this mortal life.
On any given day you may feel a slight breeze.
Perhaps it was an angel kiss if you do believe
That miracles can happen if you have the faith
Maybe it's a sad day or a special date,
That seems impossible to handle with your hurting heart.
Because someone has become an angel and you live a part
Angels are beside us on any given day.
When your surrounded by darkness they will light the way.
Angels are amazing as they float around.
Perhaps you have caught a glimpse or heard a faint sound.
Their wings a fluttering as they make someone's day.
Sharing their sweet love because they've heard you when you pray.
Believe in the everlasting and you know on day you'll be.
An angel up in Heaven that's what we need to believe.
If you live your mortal life basically free of sin
The lord makes us Angels when our mortal life does end.
So keep the faith in the Lord as you live each day
And always believe in your heart angels are
everywhere every day.

Wanda Jones
Gastonia, NC

108

Mothers

Mothers are great—that's for sure!
For anything that's wrong—she'll find a cure.
She'll share with you, she'll give up her own,
She waits to hear from you, she sits by the phone.
You tell her she worries much more than she should.
But that's because she loves you and that's clearly understood.
She's there to lend, even though she knows you may never repay.
She knows that in hell that could be a very cold day.
She never expects more than you can give—
She just wants you to be happy—be loved and to "live"
She'll cry with you when you're sad,
And no matter how old you are—she'll scold you when you're bad.
Even though you both get mad—
One day you'll come to realize—she's the best friend that you've ever
    had.
She loves your kids just like her own,
But she's still there for you when you feel alone.
She's always close—always nearby—
People just don't understand—they'll never break THIS family tie.
So treat her good—handle with care—
Let her know too that . . . YOU'LL ALWAYS BE THERE!

Karen S. Ferguson
St. George, UT

Life's Journey

As we go through life we have joy and we have sorrow
But whatever happens, we must always look at the morrow
We must be happy to just be alive
And be glad that we can survive
When you left and just went away
I just lived from day to day
But now I have a new love whom I know will be true
So I am sure that I can live without you

Lorraine Kroll
Chicago, IL

I started writing poetry in grammar school. Unfortunately, I didn't write anything for several years and then I took it up again. I am so glad I did as I can always think of something to inspire me. It gives me such a feeling of fulfillment. I like to write prose that will give people hope for a better tomorrow.

Venice Visions

I believed I lived in a island of urban paradise
The beach is near, fun to do, the weather nice.
As time has passed with a fever meanly vicious
the glowing image tarnished it's soul diminished.
Family streets, once birds sang and children played
Reeking of beer, drug deals too closely displayed
Seeking the beauty of nature's glory transplanted
Instead I find bums, gangs, and condoms discarded
Home a sanctuary of peace and tranquility should be
Is now a fortress, shuttered light, in this disharmony.
Age worn walls of artful design, lush lawns, did delight
Now prefab boring bunkers to shelter your clan at night.
Their recomposing Venice into a bizarro world sight.

Janet Freedland
Venice, CA

Seasons

Spring mornings
Flowers blooming
Temperatures warming
Birds chirping
Plant life turning green

Summer at midday
Rain showers refreshing
Butterflies gliding
Grasshoppers jumping
Children playing

Autumn afternoons
Colors changing
Cool breeze blowing
Farmers harvesting
Bonfires crackling

Winter evenings
Snowflakes falling
Icicles glistening
Families sledding
Snowmen smiling

All four seasons reflect the beauty of the world we live in and has uniquely been created by God, for us, His children. Each season shows the glory of God—revealed in His works.

Kristine Franklin
Westland, MI

The Greatest Beauty

There are many things
I call beautiful in my sight.
A starry autumn night,
birds in v-formation flight,
the array of intense color of Fall leaves,
undisturbed nature and majestic trees.
A child having fun flying their first kite,
an endless field of wild flowers,
and after a rain, a double rainbow in the sky.
Seeing good friends laughing together,
a family praying together.
An unexpected act of kindness.
So much beauty to see, I am truly blessed.

Even the cross where Jesus'
atoning blood was shed,
it flowed out of His love for us.
For the price He paid, how beautiful that was,
and "the way" was made.

The most beautiful things
my eyes will never see,
are glorified saints in the presence of Jesus forever.
I can hardly wait.
Jesus, you are the greatest beauty
my eyes will ever see.

Katrina Smith
Grady, AL

I wrote this poem while sitting with an elderly Christian woman. The important one here is Jesus—it's all about him and everything is because of him. Jesus, the Son of Man, has made it possible for all to have a heavenly destiny. By inviting him into your heart, you're spiritually born into God's family. All souls born again into his family are destined for the greatest beauty yet to behold. Trust and have faith in His unfailing word.

Pay Attention

Oh, the colors of the rainbow
how magnificent is each hue,
you have to mix them very carefully
to get the color that's true.

There are other things in nature
where God says, I love you.
So pay attention to what's around
and enjoy every scenic view,
to see how God loves and tries to please you.

Pay attention to the majesty of His work,
and give glory in His name.
He's always there to save you
and His love stays the same.

Come bask in His presence
and take pleasure in His art.
Show love for Him daily
and always keep Him in your heart.

God will show you mercy
when you do things wrong,
so we magnify and praise Him
through prayer and song.

Pay attention to the one and only God
who created everyone and everything.
So let's lift our voices now
and show how excellent we sing.

We must lift our voices
in worship and praise,
to show God we pay attention
and marvel at His ways.

Lenora M. Corbett
Reidsville, NC

King and Lincoln

Time is not important to make a warm friendship between humans
The deep feeling of a human being is the edge between ebb and flow
Movement of the stable brain, that which sways between the requirement of
the people to support each other in the worst times, in the revolution times.
It is not unique to grow the plants up on flint of life
But the stubborn thing is when we cut up plants to keep them in our hands
for a short period of time, then throw them away and run so far from them
avoiding the stench
We have the oldest body, it is tired from the loud clamor of fighting
We are tired from our big toe to the top of our head
MLK had a dream but he didn't know his bridge from the darkness to
lightness
It is not unique to have a child's plan to get peace in our side
There is no surprise if we have faith about the small details in our life
If all these events draw our footprint between us without means, distance
and variety
It is not unique for two people from different generations and life, without
meeting to fight for the common cause and without any permissions from
anybody.
Both of them were tired from the war, death, dust and clay, even though the
clay is soft and the dust is light
It is not unique for the flow to be faster than the speed of light; it's freedom
How can we measure the rate of spirit designs, approach them together, and
dance without drum
The test of freedom has a taste sweeter than honey and the smile as a baby
and soft as air
Abraham Lincoln and Martin Luther King gave the world the keys of
Heaven in the earth to open the door for all human beings to hug.

Fuzia Elkekli
Tucson, AZ

I am from Tripoli, Libya, and I've been in the United States with my family since August
2007 to pursue my Ph.D. in the Department of Geography with a major in Urban Planning
at the University of Arizona, Tucson. My five children are my flowers, and my husband is
my support forever. I graduated from Al Fateh University in Tripoli and was a professor
there. Because Arabic is my first language, I've had to learn English. I've always admired
Abraham Lincoln and Martin Luther King, Jr., symbols of freedom, because they struggled
to achieve freedom for the next generations. Freedom is like our spirit; our body without the
spirit doesn't have any worth.

Canary in a Coal Mine

There's just something missing
Some sort of satisfaction
And how do we go about fixing this?
A broke
A fix
Stifled
Relating again to the canary
I really am concerned about the bees
Out of house and home
All follow through
Nothing new
Willing myself to finish
Why don't I feel better?
Always in incomplete
Absoluteness
Why can't higher consciousness happen already?
Apparently I'm waiting right here
Finishing up

Sara Ratcliff
St. Louis, MO

My Little Sister

My little sister's name is Morgan
and she's one year old
and very bold.
Anything she sets her mind to she can do,
she plays with dolls, blocks, and loves to color.
She gives hugs and kisses, she's quite the lover.
I love to play with her until she gets mad,
then she hits me and makes me sad.
I really love her a lot though, as you can see.
She is very special to me and my family.

Madison Cosman
Hoffman Estates, IL

An October Day

I woke up early
On an October day
And opened the front door
To get on my way.

Leaves on the ground
Red, orange and gold
The wind is blowing briskly
As I shiver in the cold.

The days are getting short
And the nights are getting long
Halloween is the time
For us to sing this song:

"Trick or treat, trick or treat

My Idol Is Dead

Malcolm Forbes is dead at seventy-two,
Billionaire, financier, and publisher, too.
Leather jacket—motor cycle—discoteque—
Two million dollar party—personal check.

Visiting heads of state he traveled far and wide.
Elizabeth Taylor was often at his side.
His death was frightening to learn.
I have cause for concern.

It made me mad
It made me sad
It makes me want to cry.
Malcolm was two years younger than I.

C. B. Whitehead
Montgomery, AL

Cold, Wet Day

This poem is being written on a cold, wet day.
I sit here pondering over what to say,
About what I read and heard, about what I said and learned,
There are so many similies and metaphors, banned words and strong
    verbs.
When you write your thoughts must be clear and strong,
To make your stories amazing and long.
There are also prepositions such as above, beneath, and beyond.
Alliterations, because you busted her button you were betrayed,
But there is more, openings and closers, clauses and -ly words.
Now this poem is done, I wrote what I learned,
Now I know what to say,
And this was written on a cold, wet day.

Kayla Waycaster
Hephzibah, GA

There's No Love, Where There Is No Doubt

I know there are times when you think I don't love you
And there are times when I'm not sure if I still do
I know there are times when you feel the same
But don't be sad you are not to blame
For there's no love, where there is no doubt

When you're in love, you're a victim of circumstance
There's so many things we'll never understand
Sometimes you feel you're not loved enough
Sometimes you think you're in love too much
For there's no love, where there is no doubt

It doesn't matter how much someone loved you
You're going to have moments of despair
It makes no difference how much love there is between you
There will be times when you'll doubt the love you share
For love is like the winds that blow
That loving feeling comes and goes
For there's no love, where there is no doubt

Jerry McQueen, Jr.
Montgomery, AL

In Memory of September 11, 2001

With torch held high, the lady is crying,
For all the senseless loss and dying.
Her city is touched by such despair,
With sadness more than she can bear . . . she sheds a tear.

Her heart is filled grief, yet pride.
An empty feeling deep inside, for all of those
Who had no voice, who lost their lives without
A choice . . . she sheds tear.

And honest Abe sits silently upon his chair of stone,
Saddened by the sudden devastation of his home.
He's seen much strife in the years past, and once again
With the stars and stripes flying at half mast . . . he sheds a tear.

But in his heart deep gratitude for all the selfless deeds; the firemen,
Policemen, and citizens who helped those in need; and as the Potomac
Flows silently in his view, he prays that America will find strength and
hope anew . . . he sheds a tear.

From the streets of New York City to Washington D.C., to a field in
Pennsylvania for all the world to see; our lives were changed forever,
our will put to the test; we are now a nation in mourning, as we lay loved
ones to rest . . . we shed a tear.

But the red, white and blue still flies proudly in the wind and within its
regal beauty there is a message we must send . . . . We will stand united
for all the world to see; we are still the home of the brave and the land of
the free. We will wipe away the tears . . . but we will never forget.

Vicki Lucas
Gilbert, AZ

I Love You, Baby

I love you baby
and that will never change
even when I move on
no other will be your name

I won't leave without you
there is no way and no how
I will never go anywhere
not today, tomorrow or now.

You are my everything
and a whole lot more.
If you would ever leave me
my heart would be sore.

All of the love I have
would blacken and I would die alone
because you're my everything
The completion to our home.

I went too long before
and dated only a few guys
but none of them were you
cause constantly I heard lies.

You are my entire world
and I love you so much.
I long for your love
your every kiss and every touch.

Shalisha Cartwright
Conway, AR

I Dreamt of You

I dreamt of you one day while I lay on a hill of snow.
The flakes trickle down and touch my face just so.
I close my eyes and believe it is your gentle touch of my cheek,
    a wisp of the lips, a yearn for a kiss.

I dreamt of you one day while I lay in a meadow so green.
The rain sparkles down, not even touching the ground, and the
    absorption right through my skin, so subtle, it is begging to let you i

I dreamt of you one day while I lay in a bed of roses.
The gentle breeze places a soft caress amongst my chest and the teasin
    pleasure that is you.
The aroma in the air it is as if your right there, I can even feel the heat
    your breath.

I dreamt of you one day while I lay in a pile of leaves with the overture
    of their crackle your voice they carry with the commencement of yo
    plea, that you also want me and we are in awe of one another.

I dreamt of you one night with stars shimmering so bright, the moon
    aglow as if all must know the carnal feelings we have for each othe

For the kiss of the dew was that placed upon you and all the pleasures
    that come with it.

Barbara A. Robirds
Westphalia, MI

The Moment of Consciousness

After giving careful "thought" and with undivided attention, scrutinizing with divulgence, observations begin to call forth ideas as they step up to be named and numbered.
One called the image begins to reflect in the mirror.
I'm looking head on with full conception . . . ! With the acquaintance of understanding activity.
Weighing every "thoughtful" thought within the balance upon the scales of Justice, measuring their subconscious motives, their height, depth, every width, and length through the eye of that divine love.
And it is here that I find that "life," life to be alive, living, to be aware, breathing.
The freedom of expression, growth, purpose, and progression.
Life is the most precious!
And the most valuable gift ever given to me, my fellow man, the whole creation and the entire universe.
A treasure that not even words can explain . . . .
Time and space cannot contain.
My statement of declaration is that
"Every Good Thought that's thought of "Thoughtfully" is worth Millions! Every Good Thought highly spoken or from above "Utter verbally" is worth Billions! And is the Manifestation of Trillions!"
The Eternal moment, Golden moment, Present moment is the only moment.
And the only moment that's guaranteed, the only moment of Reality.
And it is real where you enter into the secret silence of your own consciousness there "Realizing" This is where the "Divine Lover"!

Darnell Johnson
Chicago, IL

Form and Abandon

An alcoholic haze and sexual satisfaction
need coupled two units and I was formed
1950s pregnancy resulted in marriage
lucky me—lucky us—4 more units
an entire dysfunctional family unit
fueled with alcohol and Catholic guilt
years pass, the cycle repeats
finally the original unit legally splits
Too little Too late Too much damage
First formed unit—me—
severed all communication with the male
unit in 1986—
Too toxic for my soul
My cancer in 2003 strained a deteriorating
relationship with the female unit—
broke my soul
years of therapy brought me to level—I thought
The male offspring began worshipping the
female unit this fall—
She no longer requires my assistance.
The female unit is cutting all ties to me.
I am abandoned.

Teri Mahoney
Gladstone, MO

Words Forbidden

You call it my sexual expression,
I call it immoral.
But you don't care what I think,
I can't feel pain remember?
Or is that just what you tell yourself,
To dismiss the sound of my tears.
The ones that fall hard to the wooden floor,
The ones that make it down my battered cheek.
This is all a game to you,
You throw me out like an extra piece to monopoly.
But you race to my side like a knight,
When the money in your wallet runs short.
You have no feeling,
It is I that feels at night
I feel the rips and the new scars,
I feel the bruises and the hand print on my face.
I hear the demands,
I listen to the commands.
All this for you,
And yet I get nothing but a new disease.

Lindsey Williams
Las Vegas, NV

Buried

Brilliant gold tones on light bronze
Softening the oblong shroud
The envelope that would seal forever
The lifeless form
Turned into an object

Inside your bed made of satin
Your eyes remain closed
A pillow to simulate sleep
Rests under your head
A mind finally at peace

Hands cold as ice hold onto faith
The cross you suffered on I now know
Beside you I kneel and say a goodbye
To a face I will never see again
Parts of me die

The heavy steal will take you away
Adorned on its corners with graceful lines
Depicting the Madonna holding her son
Her despair is disguised as ultimate hope
My hope sinks into despair

Harsh lines of metal form
Softened by handles held by cherubs
Messengers on a journey of faith
The dark earth to swallow you up
Heaven's on the horizon

Susan Moussa
Webster, MA

Untitled

I had stolen downstairs to witness the last ruby red sapphires
Glow and fall silent in the hearth slowly they dimmed, gradually fading away
But alas I said to myself why such a beauty and pleasure be stifled
Torn up tissue paper and scrunched up newspapers these forlorn and tragic tools
Would be all that would rekindle my sweet fire
So it could once again flood the hearth with its warm glow
With the lighter in my hand I set to work to start anew
But the first try failed smoldering to ashes
The second, the third, fourth, and fifth
Moaning in despair my heart ached to save the little burning vision of hope
Finally on the last attempt a flicker . . . a flame . . . a fire!
I rejoiced feeling happy and fulfilled a weight lifted off my shoulders
I lay and watched as a new mother watches her child
Simultaneously feeding nurturing it keeping it alive
And it was a child dancing on the ashes of old
It was life, it was new, it was hope that burned inside of me – hope
Late into the night my head drooped and my eyes shut and my body slowed . . .
I awoke early in the morning laying by the hearth—back to reality
To hurt and anguish to sorrow and despair
Questions were thrown at my face all I could do was smile to myself
And say barely above a whisper—hope
For there is always hope for those who believe
Always a radiant light at the end of the tunnel
Always an unawaring flame in the endless darkness

Olivia O'Conner
Marshfield Hills, MA

What's Left?

We live on this earth, but it does not belong to you or to me
This beautiful place belongs to the animals, mountains, and trees
When you look at this place what do you see?
A wonderful world, a place for beauty

Look at it twice so were both clear, look at this mess we created around
here
When you look at the plastic and trash on the ground
There are not enough eyes for all the trash that's around
What's important to us money, cars, guns, and war? Why the fuss?

How about peace, health, clean water, fresh air
The earth is willing to provide it, but apparently we don't care
We've taken this earth for granted too long
This earth doesn't need us, she'd be fine if we were gone

But we need her so stop doing her wrong
We better make changes don't you want a safe place to live
What about me and my kid's kids?

Numb to the future that will come without choice
So all you young people start using your voice
They say treat the earth the way you want to be treated,
But from the looks of things now we haven't succeeded

There's time I believe to make changes in our world
So please try to see past all the money and greed
And realize that the earth is all we really need

Raven Lewis
Glenside, PA

Cooking

Stir thoughts
in your stew bowl.
Turn them 'round
and 'round again.

Watch bubbles
as they float up.
In your core
you don't pretend.

Charlotte Plotsky
Palm Beach Gardens, FL

Life

Accept life's joys and
Disappointments along the way

Remember to pray for help,
And thank the Lord each and every day

We can't foresee the future ahead,
But He will guide us along the way

Keep your words sweet and kind
And your face with a smile

Take time to see the beauty around you,
Which extends for an unending mile

Ann Pagliarini
Warwick, RI

To My Daughter From a Misfit

As you lay there on your side
Your lips pouted and eyes fluttered to a close . . .
The worries make me curl inside
The demons come storming with haunting thoughts
I am not worthy to be called your mother
I am nothing but a misfit
From a dangerous life cycle
Born to a junkie
Chained to the domino theory
My child, yours will be different, I promise—
As the sun rises, and the clouds pass by
I only wake to hear you coo
My love for you can blind the sun and make the ocean shallow
I will strive to the moon to give you everything
Lonely, young, afraid, single, cold, my heart is shattered
The world is harsh
Yet I will carry you through the flames
Wrap you up in my comfort of hope
And watch you grow to be a woman
A woman not of my kind or the worlds
But full of pureness, joy, and peace.
I pray your eyes, mouth, ears, hands
Never see or feel the dangers of this world
O' Lord keep my daughter's slumber safe tonight.

Diana Fawver
Denver, CO

Breeze

She awakens each spring morning
To the scent of lilacs
Which I have carried to her,
Just as throughout her childhood
I always twirled her dollar store kites
Along behind her down the sand.
And I tagged along,
While she grew into her life.

When she goes home,
Exhausted from her day's labor,
I hear her silent cries and linger around her house,
Pushing clouds away from the waning moon
Until the sun climbs the sky
And fires the weathervane on the sagging barn.

When she crosses the frozen earth
To pick up the newspaper,
I shiver the maple's branches,
Tremble its tarnished leaves.

From time to time I lift up her skirt
When she wanders the apple orchard alone,
Just to let her know that even in her solitude
I'll always be not far away.

Kelly Pryor
Cheshire, CT

Wishing You Weren't Fishing

I was just wishing,
That you weren't fishing
And you were here with me

But since I'm still wishing,
And you're still fishing
That just cannot be

I know you're in search
Of that bucket mouth bass
And I hate to be
Such a pain in the ass

But unless you want
A fight well fought
Leave behind the ones
You could have caught

So, grab your rod,
Your reel and bait
And come on home
To your sweet mate

Then you won't be
The one to say
That "she's the one
That got away"

Kathy McFatter
Richardson, TX

Flower Power

Gurgle, bubble, splat, sprinkle.
Down water showers.
Then suddenly, up pops flowers!
Then the seasons change and rearrange.
Then comes the snow plowers!
They press a button that says, go,
And the plowers plow over the flowers
Sticking out of the snow. Then boom!
That's the end of the flowers until next spring.
The birds will sing and again you'll see
The towers of flowers.

Georgia VanDine
Moretown, VT

The Drums of War

The drums of war sound once more
Calling our youth from shore to shore
To fight in a land a continent away
Making us safer some people say
The fighting goes on day after day
While our soldiers search for a way
To fight in a war against an enemy who
Blows up a car and himself too
Every day more bombs blow up more people die
And to another fallen hero we may say our good-bye
And day after day we ask ourselves why?

Florence Knudson
Seattle, WA

Mother

Mother left this earth in 2001.
She went to be with God's only Son.
A beautiful mansion He did prepare,
For Mom and her family who would join her up there.
My life here without Mom is oh-so sad,
But I know she is happy in Heaven with Dad.
Our loved ones are patiently waiting for "us" to get there
For that family reunion with our Lord in the air.

Joann Turner
Marysville, CA

Beauty for Ashes

In the spring of sadness, when my fear has just begun,
I turn my face to the heavens and I'm blinded by the sun.
My mortal eyes can't see what lies beyond this place,
But my fears are overcome by a supernatural grace.
In the moment that we live, we've nothing now to lose,
Except what we should owe in time if life collects its dues.
So set aside your worries and look unto the sky
And know that your redemption is standing by and by.
Now in the winter of our sorrows, when they've all but disappeared,
We turn away from darkness and laugh at all we feared.
There's no more need for sorrow, as life before you flashes,
Now out of fear rises joy, and you receive beauty for your ashes.

Joleen Carter
Lorain, OH

Reaching Out Searching In

There's something so amazing
and it happens all the time.

I find my heart is heavy
and confusion fills my mind.

I'm reaching out and searching
waiting to be known,
And that's when God comes to me
to claim me as his own.

He takes away the sadness
and fills my life with joy,
The power of this moment
one simply can't ignore.

For when I'm reaching out
and searching in,
God is knocking on my door

Hello! Come in!
What is it!

Dixie Nelson
Berthoud, CO

Alone

I simply yearn for
a union with someone

But I'm this strange
soldier of solitude

My destiny's deeds
I do not dispute

Deep down inside
I am but half a soul

Wanting and willingly waiting
just to become whole

Paul DelSordo
Hicksville, NY

The Gift

You get one chance at life
Yet so many fail
To recognize our precious surroundings
Our time could be so frail

Yet it takes devastation
To make us see
The things that were there every day
Appear so clearly now to thee

The diagnosis of the "C"
Are the words you dread to hear
But in a way it's a gift
Because your loved ones become so dear

You can view it as a curse
Or take it as a gift
But bitterness and anger
Will leave you lonely and often miffed

You need to live the positive
And the lessons you will bring
Will show you and all the others
That life can be happy everything!

Donna Lackey
Southlake, TX

Gun-Runner

Yeah, I'm a gunrunner,
And contrary to popular belief,
It's a honorable profession—sorta.
But, the hours are long and the working conditions
Leave a lot to be desired.

You're on location—usually in some god-forsaken jungle
And at landing strips you've hacked from
Tangled vines, deep within the emerald-green blanket of the rainforest.

After all, someone must
Supply the needs
Of rebel forces, wherever they bleed.

And, where there's a will, there's a way,
Or a way-and-means committee
That can override the laws
That prohibit guys like me.

But, look,
At least I draw the line at
Giving guns to kids
So they can kill their folks, or maybe me?

Michael Osborn
San Pedro, CA

Passion

A cold and dreary winter's day
The icy snowflakes and the frigid breeze
A desolate and cozy cottage,
Concealed behind the hovering trees.

The interior hides a mysterious desire
A pitter patter of want and need
A steamy shower inhabits two erotic lovers
Passion and desire plant their seeds.

Woman pressed against the wall,
Water trickling down her face
Man buried in her breast
His mind is yearning for the chase.

His hands stroke her naked flesh
Her bare legs clench with sexual desire
A forceful thrust and a wailing moan
The two lost in a lascivious fire.

He thrusts again, a satisfying sigh
The falling torrent blends with seeping sweat
A piercing scream and a wild groan
All tension is released, this leaves no regret.

The coldest of nights in this frost fog
Spent in the climax of passionate infatuation
A man and a woman so lost in spiritual desire
Sleep naked and soundly, both hearts are one.

Alyssa King
Seminole, FL

I Am a Goldfish

I am a goldfish who lives alone
I swim in a fish tank I call home
I thought, wouldn't it be great
If I had a goldfish mate

One day my owner decided to go
To the pet shop and buy me a beau
In the fish tank we both now reside
With a baby goldfish by our side

I don't need an ocean or the sea
The fish tank is big enough for me
Now I am happy as can be
With my goldfish family of three

Stella Munao
Fresh Meadows, NY

Seasons in Illiniois

All around us looks clean and white,
The snow at dusk lights up the night.
How fortunate we are to have changing seasons;
God blessed us for many reasons!

We raise corn and wheat as our major crops,
And for that reason, we need moisture in winter a lot.
It conditions the soil for planting in April or May,
Then farmers add nitrogen and other chemicals to make crops pay.

In May through August with the proper sunshine and rain,
The crops mature and turn green, then brown and hopefully they are
    loaded with grain.
This time of year when everything is green,
The state of Illinois has lots of beauty to be seen.

Then comes fall when farmers start gathering crops;
Hoping to sell them and having a lot!
If the price is not high enough, they store their crops,
Then when prices are high enough they use trucks.

The trucks deliver the grain to a railroad site;
Either loading it on a boxcar or some other plight!
Now is the time when the leaves change colors,
Orange, Brown, Gold, some Green, making a beautiful scene!

Spring and Fall are the most beautiful seasons in Illinois;
Except in winter when there is snow; it's like an Artist's palette.
With gas so high, be sure and see our State;
After seeing our attractions, I'm sure it will get a high rate!

Ruth E. Allen-Clinton
Normal, IL

147

Bright Light

I am waiting for you
All I hear is the wind and
Sounds of the birds

I am missing you like
A heart needs a beat

I miss your touch
I miss your craziness
I miss the way
You held me through the rain
I am thinking to myself
Why aren't you here
When I am lonely
Missing you like crazy

Why can't I stop chasing after you
Like a dog chases its tail.
Each time I see something
It reminds me of you.
But I am blinded by this light
When this bright light goes dead
I guess it'll be my turn to move on

Rebecca Myers
Greenville, OH

An Astronauts' Poem

I was born to chase the moon and stars . . .
Not just here, but way beyond Mars.

Regardless of challenges I face . . .
I shall prevail, on a new day's grace.

In this universe of the vast unknown . . .
Someday my brave soul, may find a new home.

The failure to succeed is not always lost . . .
As the betterment of mankind, is worth any cost.

When I reach to the heavens in search of a new way . . .
Always remember, tomorrow's a new day.

Vernon Kenworthy
Phoenix, AZ

Concise

Do I not long to be cunning like the fox?
Would I not love to soar as the birds on high?
To run faster than the mighty cheetah—
or dance with the dolphin's admirous ballet?
I would, however, envy the eyes of the falcon,
rising above all, zeroing out his prey like a
needle-in-a-haystack with undaunting perception.
Truly this enhanced sense be my advantage
to foresee the many paths of error in due
advance, limiting the potential for unseen mistakes.
Had we been given these exceptional gifts,
we'd then be void of learning and overcoming
the everyday challenges; for everything
would be only too simplistic.
All being too perfect we'd eventually cease
to exist due in part to our own powers
of extremes. Settling for my supplemental
injustices instead,
To my own devices: I surrender.
Thankful in all that I am, and also for
all that I am not.

Lori Pooler
Elkhart, IN

Rune Songs

Come is the winter of frozen rivers,
And the darkness of long cold nights.
Heavy is the mist that comes a creeping
Shrouding the warmth of the brief sunlight.

Now the forests sparkle in ice cloaks,
And the deer wade knee deep snow.
Black velvet is the night sky
Lit by the northern lights eerie glow.

Home is the warrior, home from the raid,
And the geese have all flown south.
Now the bear sleeps deep in his den
Dreaming of the slow return of spring.

Lonely are the songs the wind is singing,
Mournful notes of never-ending night;
While the lore singer sings us stories
Of the hero's courageous fight.

Now the long ships stand at the quay side
Now the dragon rests through the night.
Soon the spring will return to the land
Bringing flowers like the incoming tide.

Then the armor will be polished
And the bows will be restrung.
Now the dragon ships start prowling,
Time for new heroes' songs to be sung.

Bonnie C. Sommerville
Higginsville, MO

I am a Christian and genealogist with a life long interest in Viking lore. I was delighted several years ago to discover I am a direct descendant of King Herald Bluetooth (what a visual!) of Denmark. It was King Herald who introduced Christianity to the Danes. Over the years I taught myself to write Norse Runes. I also developed a fascination with the Norse oral tradition of passing down history through the generations, and longed to write something of my own using the same ancient hauntingly beautiful, sing song style. The result was "Rune Songs."

Glorious Spring

The pansy pushed the buttercup
And said, "Come it's time to get up."
Old man Earth shed his coat of dull green
And put on a new one fit for a queen.

The blue bells came running over the hill
To dance to the tune of the whippoorwills
The shy little daisies covered with dew
Greeted the sun in a sky of blue.

The birds again sang in the trees
In rhythm with the honeybees
Of all the seasons, there's just one that brings
The beauty and splendor of a glorious spring.

Rose M. McKim
Hanover, PA

Sudden Death

Those are extremely wise and sage words you have for me.
But my heart is breaking.
I appreciate your kind words and truly believe you are right.
When will the pain stop? You don't have to answer that.
I get so angry lately at everyone and at no one.
I can hardly figure out what to do next.
I can hardly drag myself out of bed.
I fight to keep from going back to bed.
I cry constantly when alone.
I cry very hard for what we will not share.
I miss my Emil.
Cry it out.
Be angry.
Acknowledge your breaking heart.
Stay in bed.
Go back to bed.
Damn your bed.
Damn it all.
Don't know what to do—do nothing.
Regret not having your beloved Emil in all of your tomorrows.
Mourn and mourn fully.
Your grief is real and deserves to be felt—to flow.
Don't suppress your feelings—they're real after all.
Healing cannot begin until you're done mourning!
Keep your faith, your health and your common sense.

Susan I. Frank
Appleton, WI

Silence, History, and Violence We May Be

Silence injected through me
Places that I can't hide are feared
Never again will there be silence.

History has taken me away
A place where is not to be stolen
Stolen of history

Violence is all there is
Never again will there be silence

History has taken me away
A place where is not to be violence
But then again it starts off
With a history of violence injected
With silence pierced through you

Dark and cold we may be
But this is no winter now
The frozen misery of centuries
Breaks, cracks, begins to move
The thaw, the flood, the upstart spring
Comes up to face us everywhere
Never to leave us
Till we take the longest stride of soul men overtook

Jasmeen Jackson
Las Vegas, NV

I started writing poetry in the sixth grade. I never liked writing in general because of how much time it took to think of a topic. My poetry means a lot to me. I get to express myself the way that I feel so no one will know how I feel. My mom, dad, sister, and brother never read my poetry or short stories. It would be a great opportunity to see my poetry published, so my family can see what I've written. If anyone reads my poetry and asks what inspires me, I wouldn't know what to say. I just want them to understand that I am trying to get better at writing so that one day I can write my mom's and my biographies so everyone understands what or why it happened to us.

My Memory

I used to have a memory
That went most everywhere with me,
I knew a name for every face,
Now memory leaves me in disgrace!

I never used to write things down,
Not even when I went to town,
Today my memory lets me down,
Leaves me standing with a frown!

I climbed the stairs and wouldn't you know,
My memory just didn't want to go,
I retraced my steps and sure as can be,
My memory came right back to me!

Where did I put it? I just can't say,
Had it in my hands yesterday,
Could I be losing my memory?
No! That could never, ever be!

Perhaps I should take a positive look,
Sometimes memory needs to be shook,
When I think of the things I do recall,
Memory's still there, but only "on call!"

Marjorie Hamm
Wisconsin Rapids, WI

Just Come on Down

Just come on down. It would be so nice to make the coffee.
It's been many years since the children are gone.
You just don't know how happy your being here makes me!

This old house has been empty for long enough,
Since the children are married and grown.
I've got plenty of room, so bring your stuff,
Don't think twice—move in with me!

It's such a joy to have all my rooms filled again.
Come in, get warm, stay out of the rain.
What do you need, a cup of tea or some coffee?
Do you like it black or do you like it sweet with cream?

The least of these, these are my families!
The least of these, these are my families!
There are my families, there are my families!

Can I come in? My momma's hungry.

Maria Zultak
Hollywood, FL

My Words

Why is there such a disconnect?
My thoughts and uttered words are not equivalent

I have thoughts and feelings of grandeur and splendor
But my spoken words are at times appalling
I desire to be an accomplished, witty wordsmith
But I end up sounding like a fool

I struggle to regain some composure
Perhaps it wasn't so bad
People can be so harsh and cruel
But others can be very forgiving
Especially those that care

Sometimes I am right on cue
Thoughts and words intermingle
Why can't she see that side of me?

I will sit quietly among those I care to impress
Waiting for the opportune time to express
The time is right . . . oh, no . . . I did it again!

Thomas Vaculik
Poughkeepsie, NY

I don't consider myself too much of a poet, but I am a capable writer with a story to tell. Upon seeing the advertisement for a poetry contest, I thought why not put something/ anything down on paper for a change. I wrote this poem on a whim and did not spend too much time with it in fear I may never think it was good enough. Whether I win this contest or not, I feel much better that I finally took some action. Actions often do speak louder than words.

I Dreamt a Dream

I dreamt a dream . . .
Filled with twinkled eyes and inspired spirits. A fantasyland where love
was unyielding and hopes were not fatal. People slept in peace and
exhaled free of worry. They were satisfied with the words of their hearts
leading them to greatness and were open to more than just ideas, but to
means of endless possibilities that surpass lack of self-confidence.

This dream was of many sweet dreams . . .
Of bright minds best-suited for understanding. "Love me Mommy, hug
me brother," and I am reassured of this love when my hand is met with
the warmth of another. My heart sang and my stomach fluttered and I
smiled with insurmountable joy.

And then I woke up . . .
To bad dreams. Black like silent screams and dark souls that stand for
dry carelessness. I dream of dreams and live the nightmares. Forever.

Devin A. Shaw
Decator, GA

Hooked!

the 4th of December
fondly will I always remember
mesmerized . . . hooked!
in a heartbeat my world shook
little do I know
you will come again my way
one chilly fine day
pretty woman finally meeting her match?
or same as the others who just watch
you said "I got class!"
in you, I got a lifetime pass
in your eyes . . . a glimpse . . . of forever?
"being together" . . . a prayer of this dreamer
star gazing . . . wondering
is it you . . . my destiny
or just another fantasy?
life they say is like a book
what the heck . . . for now, I am utterly hooked!

Beth
Union City, CA

Friends

When the going gets tough
When we need some luck
And our future's not clear,
If we have some good friends,
Then we've nothing to fear.
But to have a true friend's love
We'll need a little help from the Lord above.
Be there when friends are sad and blue
So they'll know they can depend on you!
So, give of your time and talents,
To help your friends keep their lives in balance.
Then all of us will happier be,
Whenever a true friend we'll see!

Eleanor M. Kidwell
Horton, KS

Warmed by a Yuletide Memory

From out of his head,
the community of dead cries out
in the cold womb of night.

With voices frenetic,
the prophetic sound cuts through
the uncertainty and strife.

A new baby born to
a world undeserving tells
us that morning is here.

The gift lies unused,
cold, stillborn, abused
by a slovenly, unworthy life.

Is there still time to change,
my mind rearrange,
on this snowy, white Christmas night?

Malcom Wessing
Grand Rapids, MN

I Am

I'm glad I'm not a ball
Getting kicked around
I wish I was a waterfall
Splashing to the ground

I'm glad I'm not a chimp
Swaying on a rope
I'm glad I'm not a something um,
Oh yeah, it's called an antelope

Well I am a something
A who I what to be
I really love that something
Because that something's me

I'll tell you I'm a person
And whom I'll always be
What am I again?
Oh yeah, I'm me

Trudy Smith
Albany, CA

Jealousy the Beast

Why must we be jealous of each other?
There are those who are jealous of their brothers!
Jealous because others are better off than we,
Jealous of the world, even though we are free!
Rich envy the poor...poor envy the rich
Still both have the same future ahead!
Each of us, rich or poor, will have
Our share of happiness and sorrow,
No one knows what might happen tomorrow!
The rich may become poorer than you
Even knocking for aid at your door.
So let's give a hand, help each other
To understand that life may be short,
But still be enjoyed if we destroy
This beast who is trying to wreck
Our life and our peace!

Jennie Cerruti
New York, NY

The Environment

The environment is my friend,
Until the very end

The environment gives me warmth and pleasure,
At an amount not even I can measure!

The sweet smell of nature around us
Makes me feel very joyous.

Do you want this to last,
Or be in the past?

Look around you and tell me what you see.
Is it the smell of flowers, or a little bee?

This is what you are giving up.
Look stop and back up!

It amazes me how it all happens so fast,
That none of this will last.

We are the cause of this,
Surely its something we'll miss.

By working together we can save this planet,
And the spirit that lies within it.

So, don't pollute,
And give your salute!

Huda Aziz
Coral Spring, FL

Blind

And with your blindness
You've become so conceited.
The smiles you've faked,
And the people you've cheated.

And with your pride,
You've become so obsessed,
To make sure everyone knows,
That you are the best.

And with your new life,
You've seemed to have forgotten,
The friends you have lost,
And the troubles you've caused them.

And with your reluctance,
You've failed to realize,
The problem you're in,
And the result of your lies.

And now that you're lost,
There is no escape.
So stand by and watch,
Your words fade away in vain.

Daniel Bednarczyk
Fayette City, PA

Trust Him

My life's been rough and rocky,
At 90 I'm weary to the bone!
Yet something does sustain me;
Truly, I'm not "Going it" alone.

For here, out on life's rolling main,
In my battered little boat,
Rowing with just one crippled oar,
'Tis Jesus who keeps me afloat!

Isabel Hintzman
Chippewa Falls, WI

Peace Poem

Peace is nature without harm
Peace is men arm in arm
Peace is animals running free
Peace is kids filled with glee
Peace is waves crashing against rocks
Peace is birds in giant flocks
Peace is penguins huddling in an igloo
Peace is the sky bright and blue
Peace is monkeys hopping tree to tree
Peace is otters swimming in the sea
Peace is freedom in fresh smelled trees
Peace is all to me

Matt Vickers
Livermore, CA

All Those Years

There it is, enclosed in glass and wood.
All the years standing silent—
Against the wall.
I dare not look too closely now
For it might fall from whence it stood.

Just a passing glance is all I dare,
For to venture in that sheltered place
Might shatter the silence
Lined up with such tender care.
I'll just let it be in that protected space.

So now I leave it to that distant time
Enclosed in glass and wood.
A passing glance as I walk by
A hearts eye glimpse, that I might bask
In all those years—when time was mine.

Joan R. Dunlop

Drugs, Gangs and Guns

Drugs, gangs, guns, and bullets
We need to stamp it all out
Little children are being killed
Let us march, fight, and shout

Gangs are roaming the streets
Packing guns and selling drugs
People are being ruffed and killed
By these crack-headed gangs of thugs

So let us all join with the Police's
And fight and take out streets back
Let us clean up our neighborhood's
From all these thugs selling crack

We got to clean up our city now
And arrest and jail these thugs
Put them in jail where they belong
That's killing and selling drugs

Nancy Pannell
Brooklyn, NY

Solitude

As I sit and watch the ocean water sweep gently over the beach,
I feel all of my problems and fears wash back out to sea with the waves.
The smooth swish and calm stroke of the water slowly becomes closer
and closer to my feet.
Slowly but surely closer and closer, bringing little bits of seaweed and
particles of sand along with it.
Finally the soft strokes of the water reach my feet, causing a sudden
shock to run all through my body from the cold temperature of the
water.
The newly-dampened sand beneath my feet begins to sink a little,
but not enough to actually be noticed.
It feels soggy, yet comfortably cold, as I push my feet under the sand
and begin to wiggle my toes...
Causing the sand to clump and sink through the gaps.
I feel nothing but satisfaction, for I had moved the sand to other places
without actually wanting it to go there,
I am at peace with only the sound of the waves sweeping the beach to
hear, and a cool tingle of the wet sand on my feet to feel.

Amy Redmon
Grass Valley, CA

Change

When you look in the mirror,
What do you see?
Are you, the person, that you'd hoped you'd be?
Did you have a dream,
That just never came true?
Did you put all the blame,
On everyone, but you!
The years have passed,
And now it seems too late,
Have I wasted my life,
Have I chose my own fate?
So what happens now...,
Did I make the right choices?
Maybe, I should have listened,
To those inner voices…
They prompted me, to help one another,
To care for my neighbor, to love my brother.
If I would have listened,
To the good in my heart,
Would my life have been different,
Is it too late to start?

Greg Wright
Marion, OH

Yellow for a Soldier

The yellow ribbon reminds us
Of he who is not here;
The one of many fighting—
So we, without fear, can live.

Our security was threatened
So he went to fight—
Fight side by side with others,
For the freedoms we enjoy.

He sees the horrors of war—
The destruction left behind,
The many lives that are ended—
Yet at home the yellow ribbon of hope
Reminds us he'll come home.

We pray and hope for his return,
We look for him each day—and yet
We know he shan't return
Until his work is done.

Sarah Hovey
New Berlin, WI

Light of My Life

A cup of tea and you
A fireplace meant for two
Your arms so warm
Your lips so tender
Take my heart in sweet surrender
Times remembered
Bring a smile to my face
I hold on tight
I shiver in delight
My heart is like a flower
A bud bursting in bloom
It sings with joy when I'm near you
You lit my fire
The flames burn high
They light the way to be by your side

Barbara Spangler
Hilliard, OH

Like a Falcon

Mother, like a falcon you watch over me,
Ready to nurture when I need your care.
Beautiful and poised,
You flap away into your ever-changing domain.
Onlookers gaze upon your inspiring awe, with water-crystalled eyes.
Relaxed and peaceful,
Your mother-toned voice resonates like a falcon's soft whistle.
Angered, your voice shrieks a raging caw,
Carried by a brisk choppy wind.
Instinctively protective, you swoop down
Upon threatening prey that sneaks in your roost.
Fully grown, you nudge me off your nest,
Casting me into a worldly abyss.
Stumbling, I fall to ground like a flustered baby bird.
You, however, raise me up from the withered forest floor,
And allow me to fly freely.
Dignified, you
Sail through the grassy mellowed valleys,
And skim the southern coastal waters.
Your feathers of wisdom soar tales of your long-lasting life.
Each one lifted on new currents,
Spreading through the world,
Just as you fill me up with your motherly love.

Ryan Smithies
Pensacola, FL

Father's Day Poem

The years come and go, and the years fly by,
And it often makes me wonder why…
You chose me to be the one
To love with, laugh with, have lots of fun.

I'm so grateful we have each other,
There could never be another.

So on this very special day,
There is just one thing I have to say…
Thanks for all the things you do,
The way you love, the way you care,
The way, for me, you're always there.

So celebrate, enjoy your day,
I love you more than words can say.

Happy Father's Day from me to you,
One thing you can count on, my heart will always be true.

Jane Russo
West Islip, NY

Rose

I know a rose
    That was beautiful
And full of dreams
    Saw possibilities and
Worked to make the world better
    I know a rose that got hurt
And swore to never love again
    I know a rose that never saw
How beautiful, kind, loved she was
    I know a rose that missed out on
The possibilities around her
    I know a rose who never dreamed
Never loved, never kissed and never danced
    Until the day she passed away
I knew a Rose.

Ivie Igbinomwanhia
Bronx, NY

Mother Nature Is All

Mother Nature can be
As peaceful and calm, as a warm summer day
As gentle and delightful, as an April Spring Shower
As scary and frightening with thunder and lighting
      That chills go up and down your spine
As strong and powerful, that with one shake can crack
      The earth and destroy all that we make
As wicked and cold, as a gun shot that can kill a life
Mother nature is the creator of all and can be the
Destruction of the world
But, we the people cannot create all as Mother Nature does
But, the destruction of the world will be from us all
She is the alpha and the omega, the beginning and the end
And only part of what is to begin

Bette Stimson
Tempe, AZ

Forever More

When everything's wrong, nothing feels right. Days pass by and nothing is right. There's those minutes of happiness, and the others of pain, and nothing seems to be the same. But you can't dwell on the bad, you must think of the good. Always to remember you need to feel good. You have friends and family that are by your side, and that's when everything feels all right. It makes life easier to remember the good times and not the bad. Memories will come and go, but always remember keep your head up high and don't let the feeling show. Show your personality of how you want it to be. This is how it should be. No one wants to see you sad, not even the loved one that went bad. They go to a better place and are always at your side. They want you to do well no matter how hard you try. You must remember they left a place in your heart and no one can take that away from you, no matter how hard they try. But the memories and good times you will keep and cherish. So when you met them again it's no longer goodbyes but more of the hellos to keep in your heart forever and more.

Brianna Collins
Taylor, PA

My Miracle

When I first heard the news I sat and debated,
And now I look at him and see the miracle I created.

A beautiful smile with beautiful blue eyes,
And now I know the joy only a mother could recognize.

I wake up every morning now having a reason to live,
It took him to teach me how to stop taking and now wanting to give.

I hold him and I know I'll never love anything as much,
It's a wonderful feeling knowing only I have his mother's touch.

All my friends get to go out and party, but to me, nothing could be
    more fun,
They might have the joy of freedom, but I have the joy of a son.

I was scared to raise him alone, but his real father is missing out,
Now my fears are gone and I'm the lucky one with no doubt

The happiness I feel when he smiles at me or the sound of my voice,
Watching him sleep right now, in my heart I am so happy knowing
    I made the right choice.

Christy Mathews
Whites Creek, TN

Pie in the Sky

When I was just a small fry
I was just about knee high.
I looked up in the sky
And a pie fell from the sky
And landed in my eye.
With pie in my eye
I began to sigh.
I saw a bird fly by
And asked that bird in the sky
Why did that pie fall from the sky
And land in my eye?
And the bird replied
Silly small fry with pie in the eye,
Pies don't fly
That was a bird pie that fell from the sky
And landed in your eye.
Now with bird pie in my eye
I really began to sigh.
I told that bird in the sky
The next time that bird tries another bird pie fly-by
I'll put a mud pie right in his eye!
Now the moral of this story is
When you are looking to the sky
Wondering about all those whys.
Be careful for that bird in the sky
He might just try to put a bird pie right in your eye.

Steve A. Warren
Plano, TX

His Love Still Remains

My father meant so much to me
In so many ways,
And I will miss him forever,
Especially on this, my wedding day.
I wish that he could be here
For I long to see his smile.
I wish that he could give the bride away
And walk with me down the isle.
I wish that he could touch
My children's lives
As he has so dearly touched mine.
My heart aches, for he ran out of time.
But while he was here
He brought laughter and smiles.
He gave me confidence
And so much love—if only for a while.
He gave me encouragement
And unconditional love,
And I know he is still watching
From somewhere up above.
His love still remains,
And though I have lost so much,
I will forever be thankful
For all that I have gained.

Rachelle Brown
Howe, TX

Minnesota N'ice

December nineteen, two thousand seven,
Landscape exposes, a frosty white heaven.
Everything white, for wildlife quite barren,
Nothing but empty to reach up and scare'em.

Air crystallized, degrees up to nine,
Birds flutter out from tangled-up vines.
Tree trunks bare, all in a line,
Memory reminds of summer's green time.

White sparkling branches, nature's own jewels,
Scattered all over with no latent rules.
I sit here amazed on my creaky white stool,
What a grand way to welcome the Yule.

I toast you, Jack Frost, and all of your friends,
Sun, water and moon a christmas card send.
Gleaming glass ice clings to the end,
Creating more beauty around each little bend.

Warm winds storm in, relentless and mean,
Destroying the beauty of this marvelous scene.
Falling white angels, frame nature's great scheme
Happened so fast, now just a dream.

Doug Bultman
Spicer, MN

I am a retired businessman living on a 5,000 acre lake in central Minnesota. The area is very rural which means we live very much in concert with nature. The poem I submitted was a verbal picture of a foggy, very frosty, and beautiful morning just before Christmas. The beautiful landscape glistening appeared and disappeared in less than one hour. Most of the poetry I write is about my surroundings, including people, places, and events. I also write many poems with humor about senior citizens.

When Darkness Encamps

The darkness encamps and blocks the view
It's just the path that he takes us through...
Bumpy walls with thick dark smoke
Is that a light at the end of the road?
Razor knives beneath our feet
It's getting hot, no time to sleep.
Suction cup entangles the mouth
Hammers pounding heavily against the heart
Peeling the skin from the inside out
Leaving only scars that never
Seems to depart...

Anna M. Pasigan
Louisville, KY

Lost Love

I look into the darkened sky,
and wish upon a star.
I close my eyes and think of you,
and wonder where you are.
In my thoughts I see your eyes,
as blue as a summer sky,
we're dancing on a balcony as time slowly passes by.
Together we're as strong as any bond can be,
my heart and soul belong to you and yours belong to me.
So many stars up in the sky as I close my eyes this night,
to dream of you and miss your love until the morning light.

Betty R. Hall
Columbus, OH

Crossing the Street

The fall wind scattered brown leaves about the street
as the turtle-faced old man hobbled along
with a cane in his right hand.
He was bent over, his nose nearly touching his chest.
The gray-haired woman by his side smiled at him
as they approached the crosswalk.
He reached over and took her hand
and they crossed the street together.
A young couple followed closely behind them.
The young man muttered scornfully at the old couple's slow progress.
The young woman at his side glanced at him
and shook her head disapprovingly.
More leaves fell from the trees beside the walkway
and were whisked about as the sun slowly sank in the west.
Flowers were dying in the garden beside the nearby houses,
and milkweed parachutes from a nearby field
landed in the road and on the sidewalk.
These white seeds carriers amused the old couple
as the young couple hurried past them.

Gerald A. Davis
Epsom, NH

Everything You Are

You are our sunshine
When we are cold
You are our strength
When weakness shows
The most beautiful snowflake amidst all the snow
The most colorful leaf the wind doth blow
The brightest star shining above in the sky
The loveliest of flowers that bloom with no reason why…
A dewdrop that kisses the flowers each morn
The cry of a baby that has just been born
Quiet of evening when all is calm and bright
A butterfly kissing your cheek at night
Your smile that brightened even the gloomiest day
Big brown eyes that sparkled and lightened the way
Words that were spoken that were cheery and true
These are just some of the ways we will remember you…
We miss you dearly, our lovely Shawntae
For you are our morning, our night, and our day
Your laughter and humor will always be free
You will be in our hearts for eternity…
We know you are with us wherever we go
We love you and miss you… just want you to know…
All our love forever…

Joyce Connell
Fort Collins, CO

186

Untitled

My absent wife's cat sits beside me
In companionable silence,
Silent, as only he can be.

We've talked a lot, the two of us,
Me explaining that she's gone,
While he listens, silent and contained.

I tell him she won't be back,
And that we're alone.

His silence answers me,
Echoing through silent rooms
And in my silent heart.

Dennis D. Nelson
Andover, MN

Writer's Inspiration

If the desire to be a writer
lingers in your mind.
Then give it a try,
no telling what you may find.
Many knacks
go undiscovered,
with talents hidden
until uncovered.
You must pay the fiddler
if you want to dance.
Success will elude you,
until you take that chance.
Your first efforts
may not be bold and gallant.
With hard work and faith,
you can polish your talent.
Seek the Almighty's
help in prayer.
God's at your side,
He's always there.
Waiting for inspiration
you put off trying until later.
Then you won't become a writer,
but always be a waiter!

Myron R. Fischer
Ferdinand, IN

Our Embrace

Sitting near the window,
I'm comfortable in my chair.
It's a cloudy, warm summer afternoon.
I'm here all alone, then he comes to me.
The wind.

Gently, softly; he whispers to me.
Slowly moving my hair away from my neck
he kisses me sweetly.
I enjoy every moment of his presence.
Another kiss.

Changing his position, now he faces me.
He strokes my cheek and I close my eyes.
Next, a light caress of my bare shoulders.
All the while, he whispers warm words of love.
I smile.

Rising, I stand before him.
Surrounded by gentleness and warmth,
his presence envelopes my body.
I've awaited this loving encounter.
Our embrace.

Sandra A. Healey
Plymouth, MI

Purpose

We work hard eight hours a day;
Living each second exactly the same way.
We stretch each dollar and pinch every cent;
Still, there's barely enough for rent.
Like an unbloomed flower we try;
What's the purpose, does anyone know why?
The purpose is for praise and success;
Nothing more and nothing less.

Sandra Lee
Washington, D.C.

Never Purchase Soul on Credit

As I was climbing the tree of life
With soul duly purchased—cash and carry
(Never purchase soul on credit)
I stumbled, did not fall, slipped and maintained control;
Saw Abe ascend to the canopy;
As did Martin.
When you get it right you go to the top.
Ascending the tree of life requires courage,
Knowledge, skill, and above all, discipline and focus.
Some make the ascent while others attempt
And some just stand holding soul purchased on credit
Not even looking up.

Arthur J. Hayes
Temple Hills, MD

I Am Ready

I stand here
On the battlefield,
Suited in uniform
With gun in hand,
Sworn in belt,
Canon by my side.
I am ready to fight
For our country—
The red, white and blue!

I stand here
In the sanctuary,
Clothed in suit and tie,
Unarmed,
Bible by my side,
Hands lifted up
To Heaven.
I am ready
To give praise
To our Lord—Most High!

Cheyenne Carroll
Binghampton, NY

Sit With Me

Sit here with me—
I desire you near.
For there's
No place I'd rather be.

The vision of your face
I've yearned to find.
Mystic beauty—a spiritual reflection
of a living God so kind—so kind.

We'll hold hands tenderly
for lengths of time—
sensing rhythmic hearts beating
as one—yours with mine.

Comfortably embracing the other
by our engaging fashion—
flowing naturally—as a sterling stream—
refreshing, yet with passion.

Blissfully, I feel your sweet presence
as indulgent as sipping Tuscany red wines
or feasting on French cuisine—
Drenched in Mediterranean sunsets—so fine—sublime.

Sit with me—me with you
Touching soul to soul—
For there's no place in all the universe
I'd rather go!

Betty C. Arnett
Louisville, KY

Pledge of Love to My Fiance

Your poet's profile thrills me,
The warmth of your embrace.
Your arms so sweet and yet so strong,
The softness of your face;
Your shoulders which I love to touch,
The need for your expression and privacy of space.

I am learning to respect you.
To give you shelter and a place
To come home whene'er you need me,
Understand and not deface
Those things you need to talk about;
Inspiring and not base.

Someday soon I'll marry you;
Be wedded in off-white lace,
Forget our pasts behind us,
Leaving sadness with no trace;
Upon our smooth soft-set brows;
And our happy futures chase.

Old slewfoot is defeated!
I know that is the case.
For I feel that Jesus changed you,
Leaving love in anger's place).
I pray that you will always love me
see pain and woe erase.

Lucille Weinstein
Brooklyn, NY

What Am I?

What am I?
I am the skeleton in your closet
That never disappears.
I am the blood you taste in your mouth
When I come near.
You grow nervous and lost when I arise.
You live in guilt and fear when I hide.
There are things that only I can make you feel.
To the point when you dread and say I'm not real.
But you are the one who chose me above all.
You sacrificed the truth and never planned to fall.
You could forget about me, I am not your friend.
And yet, I will always be remembered in the end.
Lies.

Stephanie L. Saum
Kinsman, OH

Irene

If you tell me that I have to choose something about you I will choose
your heart. Although your smile is tender I only want what makes you
tender, although your lips are seductive I only want what makes you
seductive, although your eyes are fascinating I only want what makes
you fascinating, although your face is beautiful I only want what makes
you special for myself and that something is your heart because it is the
most wonderful thing about you.

Victor C. Pinto
Brooklyn, NY

Music

I remember learning the theory,
    getting to know the basics.
I remember playing the clarinet for the first time
    and all the squeaks I uttered.
I remember my fingers falling on the white keys
    as I learned the piano.
I remember the pride of using my voice as I learned to sing,
    using a natural part of me.
I remember my emotions churning as I play the music.

I will always remember the music.

Jeffrey Ruffcorn
Chandler, AZ

Italian Adagio

When I am old
When I am truly old
I will remember bare feet on warm tiles
White butterflies dancing above the lavender
A songbird hiding in the chestnut wood
Swallows in playful combat above the pool
Hill towns glittering in the valleys
Shooting stars falling through a velvet sky

Who will remember with me
When I am old
When I am truly old?

Carol Chrissis
New Smyrna Beach, FL

Time Traveler

It's sixty-four degrees at one eleven
We've found our little piece of heaven
Warmer now than in days past
Loving the beauty that will forever last
That beauty abounding forever more
To this Heaven there's an open door
Though passing through some don't see
The place that was made for you and me
This hometown so beautiful this morning
And horns blast to give fair warning
Life now stirs ever so slight
Staying ahead of the coming night
Time passes by tick tock, tick tock
Seconds drifting by in front of the clock
The warmth of the air is so pleasing to me
Searching for my loved ones forever to be
Time traveler in a distant land
Knowing that time is at hand

Jeff Lea
Shelbyville, KY

My Heaven

Bred of fear and fleet of foot, a steed stands.
Mutual respect and virtue is a must.

I take courage to approach rein in hands.
How does a creature sense threat or trust?

Horse is a spirit I teach with hope.
Ride the path to the meadow and gentle slope.

Hoof beat by hoof beat, with a capable urge to float,
Flushed from the thicket, a doe rustles . . . I cope.

Up the steep canyon above the tangled underbrush,
A paw to the ground, whirling around, fear is a feast.

A gentle voice, a leg to his side, a hush,
An alliance of strength and steadfast quiets this beast.

Into the vast blue sky of brightness, I meet. . .
My Heaven . . . galloping beneath the saddle seat.

Helen Botsford
Antioch, CA

Maybe There Will Be a Tomorrow

Maybe there will be a tomorrow
When life is full of all the despairs
Maybe there will be a miracle awaiting
Because we have hope everywhere

Yes, there is hope for a tomorrow
Of each day we can all believe
That someday, somewhere we may conquer
This long, long dreadful disease

We go through life never complaining
Of all the things we have been dealt
But where there is hope and faith awaiting
We know that we can always stand the test

Yes, there's hope for a tomorrow
Of each day we can all believe
That someday, somewhere we may conquer
This long, long dreadful disease.

Bill Crowder
Fort Smith, AR

I am a retired school teacher and nine years as a public school football, basketball, and baseball coach. I was selected into the Hall of Fame at the University of Oregon and the National Baseball Hall of Fame of Junior College. I have served two terms as the President of the Sarcoma Club, service to mankind. As President, I worked with the Special Olympics and the Supporters of Children with Life Threatening Illnesses. The inspiration for this poem was not only my grandchildren but all youngsters with terminal illnesses.

Suddenly Old

Recently, somehow, without realizing, I turned old;
Didn't have a clue, never saw it coming, wasn't even told.
It started very slowly, could hardly call it real;
Just a little pain at times, only the lower leg, mostly in the heel;
The only pain in either knee came only when rising from the floor;
Not so bad, nothing to worry about, only a twinge, nothing more.
The small pain in my back, not noticeable until I sat up or turned;
And the pain in my neck, only in the morning and it seldom burned.
Hale and hearty, young at heart, seldom gave those pains
a second thought;
Too busy living to even think about what Old Man Time had wrought.
Just a sprain or twist I told myself, only temporary, it won't last;
If I only take it easy, go slow, watch my step, it will pass.
The doctor said it's all okay, go home and take some pills;
Just a little rest and exercise will ease your many ills.
Couldn't understand why my motor seemed to run so slow;
Still felt "great," had lots to do, many places yet to go.
Harder and harder to get out of bed, just couldn't understand;
Everything was harder, even some tremor in my hands.
Then suddenly, 2008, and the bells went off in my head;
And I knew the time was here, the time of worry and dread.
All at once, without fanfare or warning, a new year sprung;
All of the signs, the aches and pains, trying to tell me
I was no longer young.
Another year, come and gone, turning my blood cold;
Poof! Just like that, in an instant, I really have turned old.

Jerry John
St. Anthony, MN

Goodbye, My Friend

I remember being your almost neighbor.
Our younger days are long behind us.
We would play until night in the yard.

We would take up the front porch of our childhood toys.
We would dance and laugh and run around.
We would fawn over our favorite boys and dress like our favorite girls.

Then things changed, we started to grow, wearing make-up
and more grown up clothes.

Sleepovers were spent playing goofy games and laughing until morning
over something incredibly spontaneous.

But now things are different.
We have different lives and we had to go our separate ways.
I didn't want it to end the way it did.

I wish you all the luck and happiness in the world.
I hope you get all that you wished for in your future.
With this said, goodbye my friend.

We've had a lot of fun but now it's ended and we've separated.
Go get everything you've wanted and maybe down the road
we'll meet up again.

Goodbye my friend I wish you all the happiest birthdays and the merriest
of Christmases and the happiest of New Years.

Goodbye my friend.
If in any situation where you need a friend, I'm willing to put everything
behind and I'll be there for you like always.
Goodbye my friend and have a nice life, I'll see you around.

Samantha M. Shay
Pottsville, PA

My Mother's Hands

When I was born, I was lovingly embraced by my mother's hands.
When I was tired, I slept in my mother's hands.
When I was hungry, I was fed by my mother's hands.
When I was sick, I was nursed by my mother's hands.
When I was hurt, I was given a cookie made by my mother's hands.
When I cried, my tears were wiped by my mother's hands.
When I giggled, I was tickled by my mother's hands.
When I was naughty, I was disciplined by my mother's hands.
When I played, I was taught right from wrong by my mother's hands.
When I walked to kindergarten, I felt safe holding my mother's hands.
When I folded my hands in prayer, I modeled my mother's hands.
When I thought no one liked me, I was comforted by my mother's
    hands.
The years have passed and her hands may be worn;
Yet the love never changes and remains in my mother's hands.

Sharon Reinert
Brooklyn Park, MN

Music

Her hand in mine, we held hot hearts,
The blood dripped down our fingers,
Steamy on the sidewalk.
Ethereal, we slipped between each other,
I inhaled her closed eyes, panting breath,
I fed her frozen blueberries,
Coated in relief and release,
Sweet like her mouth,
Hard like our bones,
We broke them between our teeth.

Lily Haas
Chicago, IL

O' Say Can You See

O' say can you see the soldier's eyes knowing not what's awaiting him
or her.
O' say can you see the worry on his or her brow.
O' say can you see the soldier's family as he or she leaves for war
knowing that he or she may not be back.
O' say can you hear the prayers of friends and family, and when he or
she returns their prayers are answered.
O' say your thanks when you see a combat veteran who makes your
"FREEDOM" possible.
Remember—some gave all and all gave some.

Lester Viator
New Iberia, LA

The Perfect Gift

What, oh, what shall I buy?
The perfect gift to make you sigh.

It's that time of year,
The one to buy gifts for those who are dear.

It must be just right,
I will hunt day and night.

Could it be a bike,
Or something else you'd like?

Would it be a doll,
Or something really tall?

I just don't know.
I'm thinking of a package with a shiny bow.

I've searched up and down the isles.
I've looked for miles and miles.

I've seen a thing here and there,
But nothing that shows love, kindness, or care.

The one thing I now know,
What I seek is not a package with a shiny bow.

The perfect gift can't be boughten,
And never will be forgotten.

After all, the perfect gift is not silver or gold,
But is my love for you to hold.

Megan Boyles
Hays, KS

I am a Senior attending Fort Hays State University in Hays, Kansas. My poem "The Perfect Gift" was inspired by many searches to find the exact right Christmas gift for my family and friends. So many times I went shopping, just to realize I could never find the one perfect gift I looked for. I started thinking maybe I couldn't buy that perfect gift after all. Possibly it was more than purchasing something in a store. So, for all who read this: remember, the perfect gift is not something to buy, but actually our love given to all.

Trick and Treat

Mother Nature dressed herself as autumn
as she passed out her treats on Halloween.
Light frost had grayed her hair just days before,
but when I knocked on her garden door
she offered a quart of plump red raspberries—
—ready to be picked.
I had gone for Swiss chard and beets
since our clock had recently been set for winter.

In my sweats (shirt and pants for jogging),
I anticipated the picking trick—
a chance to bag and share fall bounty,
surprising neighbors and friends.
The berries, though, were my Halloween surprise,
jeweled there—and shining in late October's sun.
A better treat by far than candy bars
or gummy bears for aging goblins such as I.
It was enough to light a pumpkin smile
and scare the winter ghost away.

Ruth Naylor
Bluffton, OH

Milk, Eggs, Cheese, and Butter

Milk, eggs, cheese, and butter
A necessity for all mothers?

Coupons to clip make you buy two
A lot of times when you are through.

Dinner and movies a thing of the past,
Just a single mother trying to make it last.

No home phone or Internet,
Just one more thing to put me in debt.

Free movies at the library, who would have guessed?
Always on this saving money quest.

Child support—this week—maybe not.
I can never rely on what's in my pot.

Counting pennies, now I pick them up
For the fear of bad luck.

Through it all, you never know
What the money fairies will bestow.

The brighter side don't cost a thing,
A hug from a child, a bird that sings,
The I love yous, job well done,
I have only just begun.

Debbie Lambert
Gaies Ferry, CT

My Horrible Dream

I miss you, Tyler, very much today
All I do is always pray
Why did God have to take you so soon?
I feel like I'm on a moon
I should have said something when you were small
I feel like a big fat ball

When I had that dream of you dying
I felt like I was up high flying
Nobody would believe me if I told them
They would think I was lying
You were only four months old when I had that dream
Now I feel like I'm going to scream

I should have said something but now it's too late
I feel like I'm losing my faith
I never told anyone about my dream
Because if I did they would probably scream
I feel like I'm trapped in a hut
If I told them they would think I was nuts

Sharon A. Savitski
Bethlchem, PA

Farewell to My Dearest Friend

We have traveled many roads together, you and me,
Some on land, some in the air, and some by sea.

And in the book of life that you and I have shared,
Life dealt some ups and downs, it didn't matter, we cared.

We laughed a lot through the years,
And, yes, along the way shed some tears.

But nothing ever stopped us from having fun
And those will be my memories until my life is done.

Now your life has come to an end
I will miss you so very much, my dearest friend.

Dorothy Galloway
Gainsville, GA

The Dream in the Night

They come as they are
with their hopes from so far.

It might be through sand
or somebody's land.

They walk in the night,
it might not be light.

But they fight with the right
for your hopes of tonight.

So as soon as it's bright
and there in the light

The fight will ignite
for the right to survive

In a land so alive.

Nicolas Montanez
Bronx, NY

The Heart

The heart is the key
To everything you love.
To the things you hate,
and the heavens above.

Your heart stays true,
While your memories may fade.
Dreams begin to scatter,
Day after day.

But stay true to yourself
And your heart will never fail.
Stay true to your friends,
And you'll always prevail.

The past is the past,
Leave it where it's supposed to be.
Your heart is the future,
Your heart is the key.

Your heart knows all,
Your heart is true.
Make sure to choose your own path.
Don't let the path choose you.

Arsenio Vance
Fort Myers, FL

Heartbreak and a Shot

I'm a walking zombie with my head in the sky,
Nobody wants me and I don't know why.
Am I ugly or just an unlikable guy?
When I lost my love, I lost my life,
So I sit up at night, trying not to cry,
Thinking I'll find love again if I just try.
Lately, I think I try too hard.
It seems my life is always fast forward,
Work all week, get that money,
Get paid, get drunk, go to the club to find a honey.
Evidently that's not working for me.
Instead, I find more hoes,
End up a drunk with nice clothes.
But now I'm trying my best to be better,
So just maybe the girl I seek, I might just get her.
Instead, a drunk fool with a lot of hoes,
A good guy with a good girl, before I get too old.
These are just thoughts in my mind.
In the real world you never know what you'll find.
Hell, tomorrow you might wind up dying.

Melody Gill
Nashville, TN

Addicted

A simple touch from him was a sensation unlike any other
The taste of his lips, delectable beyond all stretches of the imagination
It is hard to live life without him by my side
Seemed as if all I'd ever need was right in front of me.

Sweet love, my obsession more like an addiction
Taking over my body, delving deep into my soul
Eventually reigning over my life.
Now as things got deeper by the day
Turning back . . . impossible.

But then again who would want to?
This uncontrollable desire to have him near
Brings back memories
Sweeter than anything else I have ever known.

He is my drug, my quick fix
What gets me through the day.
Any problem I had
Was solved whenever I'd lay eyes upon him.

When we were together
Time was non-existent.
Never did even a thing seem to matter.
The hours melted into days and days to weeks.

No matter what we will always have an attachment to each other.
We have the ultimate bond no one or anything can break.
You'll always have a little piece of me and I of you
Now and forevermore.

Tawanda Smith
Hazleton, PA

The World Financial Crisis

There is a financial crisis around the world. People are losing their
home. The stock market crash. Paying more for less on food. A nation
struggles. Inflation is raising Wall Street meltdown Republican and
Democrat need to come together in agree soon. Is this the new century
Great Depression? Too many failures of a country with great potential
as of the story of Robin Hood; he stole from the rich and gave to the
poor. American cases steal from the middle class and give it to the
wealthy American. US taking care of everybody since the first World
War share the wealth. No one takes care of us. We are losing money to
an expensive war. The world leaders meet with no solution, no progress.
Who should be held responsible? The president, congress, the United
Nation (UN)? This recession has to end. Will it be now soon or will
it continue? Is the world bankrupt? As 2009 approaches will we see a
brighter tomorrow or maybe a big black hole? The citizens of Iraq would
be rejoicing. Our enemy will have been defended. The US victory
would be to return home. We are in our own financial crisis. When we
overindulged ourselves, borrowing some money from big corporation
like Enroe Government assistance is for the people and by the people,
not for the Dow Jones or Nasdaq. Depending on the economy allowing
company to go overseas. The stock market is a gambling risk. Whether
you're in a small town or a big city don't depend on the economic
stimulus package. This financial crisis lives within your means that goes
for every walk of life.

Jennifer McLaughlin
Washington, D.C.

Love's Past and Future

I love you now
I loved you then
I will love you when
Time comes to an end.

I planned to love you
I planned to keep you
I never planned to leave you
But time stands still until the end.

Kathleen A. Ryan
Castro Valley, CA

Caring

Caring for someone is like love you always want to smile and show caring into trusting brings happiness from the above when you believe in God and you.

Doing right by others into life you will reach your goals so caring for someone always let it show and to be known caring is nice and it beats being alone.

Tracey R. Howard
Detroit, MI

Time to Open the Door

A frail flower sits
In a chair
In the sun
There anticipating when
His life will be done.

Knowing the beautiful place
Where he will be
And pain is no more
Yes, my frail flower
It's time to open the door.

To have things the way they were
Before it all began
Where you can, once more,
Be a fine figure of a man.

Leslee Murphy
Madison Heights, MI

Grandma's Gift

We have come here today to receive this gift.
So hushed and still as the lid we now lift.
The attic is dusty, but this trunk is clean
For wrapped in this box is Grandma's dream.

A beautiful quilt, each piece lovingly stitched by hand.
We gently lit it up and we start to understand
Different colors and shapes, such a beautiful sight.
Grandma is here in the threads bound so tight.

Every piece of her quilt has a story of it's own
A dream, a wish, her life becomes known.
We each hold it closely, than pass it around.
Each square has a memory waiting to be found.

Her heirloom of knowledge will live on
And our children's children will be drawn
To the warmth and love of her past days.
For with this knowledge their foundation is laid.

So thank you Grandma for this gift of love
We know you are watching and smiling from above.
This quilt of your life we shall always cherish
And our love for you shall never perish.

Debbie Wagoner
Louisville, KY

Homeless Man

There was an old man walking down the street,
His clothes was ragged, had no shoes on his feet.
His hair was long and his beard was too,
Walked up to me, said how do you do.
You got a little change a nickel or a dime,
Whatever you can spare will be just fine.
I gave him what I had, and this is what he said,
This will be enough for some milk and bread.
As my heart went out to this homeless old man,
I am so glad to be a helping hand.
So I shook his hand to be his friend,
And I hope we will be to the end.
As we both went our separate way,
I thank God for this special day.

Larry Crawford
Greenville, SC

I have been writing poetry for about two years and I enjoy it very much. I was inspired to write this poem because of the large number of homeless people across our land, a large number who are homeless in the area not far from our home. I know that I cannot help them all but I feel very blessed to have been able to share with some of them and to let them know that I care and that God loves them very much.

The Shore

Take me to the shore today,
Where old homes of mussels lay,
And the waves stroke the sand
While pipers play.
With the air caressing my flesh
I leave footprints that only a god can see,
And this is where I want to be.

John W. Brown
Tallahassee, FL

Home

Home is where the heart is.
The place where your thoughts are safe.
Home is where your family is.
Where love and caring takes place.

A home is the place you stay in.
A place where you feel secure.
Home is at the top of my mind,
While I walk out the school door.

A home is a house filled with love.
A home always has an open door.
A home never has an empty space.
That is why it is my favorite place!

Christie De Vito
Lake Ariel, PA

Gotta Get Away

Gotta get away!   Turn the cell phone off!
Go!   Go!   Go!   Until   I   want to stop!
Do   something   different   do   something   new
Maybe ride a horse   or   put on   dancing   shoes.

It's a toe tappin,   finger snappin,   crazy kind of day
Get out of my way!   Gotta get away!   Do things my way
Gotta spread my wings and breathe some country air
Gotta feel   the wind   blowing in my hair.....

Gotta get away   from this daily grind
Even if only   in my mind
Need to get out of here   just as fast as I can
Gotta get some sun   run barefoot in the sand

Rain is playing a tune   on the window pane
A train   in the distance   is calling my   name
God's majesty   shouts   from the mountain top
You can see it   all   from your fishing spot.

Charlotte K. Stoker
Mesquite, TX

Shadows

You can live today or live in your past. Today is your future, but what if tomorrow never comes? Then today will be your past. Now is the time to make your life right. If today you take your last breath, can you say The Ten Commandments and know all is well in your heart for when you meet your maker? You will have to account for all your actions in your life. In richer or poor, in sickness and health. Did they walk out of your life or did they stay?

Will your legacy be a legend or will it be grief? Did you or will you hurt someone before or after you're gone? Did you do your best? Will the person you promise to take care of be taken care of? Will they remember you with happiness or will it hurt too much to remember you at all? Words leave a scar. God can help them forgive you. But the hurt will be there until they die. Will there be tears when you're gone?

Those little things that you got mad at, was it really big enough to make the hurt you left? Take a Sec. Is the life you have lived and the things you have done, That's what, you want to be remembered for?

Before you close your eyes tonight and if you don't wake to see tomorrow, is your life in order? Have you done your best? You will have to answer to God. But have you made it right with the rest? What do you want to be remembered for—the bad you have done or the happiness you have left behind? The forks in the road you have taken were up to you. Did you take the roads God wanted you to? Think of the things you have done, for this is the only thing you will take with you when you go.

Marilyn Blackwood
Kalamazoo, MI

221

Heaven and Earth

From Womb of God to mother's womb to full emergence into light
A new soul is welcomed with every newborn's first lusty cry
And God's presence within us is acknowledged.

Life's goal is to breathe and grow in union with our Creator
Who provides sustenance, nurture, guidance
To help us find and practice those rhythms that resonate within.

· When we have grown in wisdom, goodness, and compassion
God will be seen in acts of human kindness and mundane miracles
And we will know that Heaven is all around us and in us.

And when our time in this corporeal world is complete
Our essence will become one again with the Breath that begot us
And Heaven in all its mystery and wonder will finally be fully revealed.

Anne B. Broussard
Lafayette, LA

Untitled

The broken pieces of glass
That cut my feet are jagged.
They tear and shred me into pieces.
My calloused heart filled
With memories of you.
Cauterize my wounds.
The times I remember you
I'm filled with pain and regret.
The loneliness fills my heart
Sweeps me up and carries me to a place unknown.
Laughter and smiles
Cut into my body.
I can't have that again.
And I remember
The crunching of metal.
The night filled with screams.
Skids.
You're gone.
Only tire marks remain
Of your last day.

Stephanie Jones
Montgomery, AL

So I Say

I did not know what a mother meant
Until I lost mine
My mom was the greatest
Person life had to offer and yet
Death was the only means of this realization.
SO I SAY
Mom I loved you
More than life itself
There are no words
To express how I felt.
SO I SAY
I am today what you
Have made and will
Be tomorrow what you
Have left.
I am the off spring of
Our Ancestors and the
New Generation in life.
SO I SAY
I will fulfill my life the
Way you have wished and
Accomplish my dreams the
Way you have wanted.
I saw you today
Tomorrow I won't.
SO I SAY
Fear, regrets, anger, frustration
All I felt
And still today!
SO I SAY—Miss you, Mom!

Nereida Napoleoni
Brooklyn, NY

China Doll

Like a china doll,
you keep me on a shelf.
Won't let anybody touch me,
you keep me to yourself.
But when you don't want me,
my fragile heart breaks.
Treated like a toy,
how much more can I take?

Simply for the company
you take me out to play.
You promise not to break me,
but my love you toss away.
You love that I'm around.
You say I mean so much.
In order to feel loved,
I need to feel your touch.

You don't like it
when others try to touch me,
but you find no problem in hiding me
when you go out and play.
You make me watch you play with other dolls
and expect me not to care,
because as soon as they leave you
you know I'll still be there.

You tell me we're having fun.
You want me to just relax.
I want to believe you care.
You promised to take the very best care of me
but ever since you got me
you've been silently hurting me.
Everyone is fragile—strength I lack.

With loyalty I sit there
I'd never leave your side.
But my smile is fading,
trying not to lose my pride.
I wish I could tell you every feeling I have,
but I'm just a china doll—
A convenient friend to have.

Brianne DiPrima
Utica, NY

The Gates of Bliss

From the beginning, in the days of old,
Only one place has stood bold.
Through those of wickedness, murder, vice, and greed,
This place has no need.
Possess in thou heart not any distrust,
For behind these gates is no lust.
Today is the day I surrender my sword.
I give it justly for the great reward.
I choose paradise above all to depart,
For surely in my heart, there Christ is impart.
Christ, I call You, I beg to be free,
I desire Your mercy, I beg to serve Thee!
My life is not over, it has just begun,
Since the Lamb was slain, your new life has been won.
This is the being I yearned to live in.
It has no iniquities. It has no sin.
I approach the gates of gold, behold who is near?
None other than Christ, my Savior who brought me here.
He took my hand and led me in.
There, I shall dwell, forever within.

Grayson Ostermeyer
Fort Wayne, IN

Promoted

We're students of the Master,
Who paved our way with love.
Our goal is to be promoted,
To our heavenly home above.

We know the greatest teacher,
Who sits upon His throne.
He loves us as we are,
But convicts us when we're wrong.

The school of life is difficult,
Divided, we will fall.
But add His love undying,
Then the blessings are multiplied for all.

Our time on earth is limited,
Therefore we must prepare,
If we want to be promoted,
And spend eternity up there.

The entrance exam is easy,
When the Master enters your heart,
And on that great Graduation Day,
From earth you will depart.

We'll be promoted to heaven.
No more burdens, pain or strife.
We'll graduate with honors,
And share with God eternal life.

Evelyn Rushing
Eagle Lake, FL

Mud

I see it now!
His plan!
I learned it from
My artist palette.

When I mixed all
My colors together
They made mud!

That the Lord did,
So that when we stick
A flower, tree, or
Shrub into it,

They bring back out
Of the mud,
The colors of the
Rainbow!

Mary Ann Carrico Mitchell, R.N.
Campbellsburg, KY

To Remember Those Who Sacrificed For Freedom

Thousands of miles a cross the ocean
in the strange country side,
our brave soldiers died.

For the freedom and the liberty
and for those—who cry for help.

How sad it is to see them cry
as they march with pain and dirty,
from Town to Town to kill the enemies—
as the bullets fly by and the grenades explode,
how sad it is to see them die.

But they march and march
to the end on the road,
tired and hungry with the spirit—
and the victory for all of us.

Otto Valnoha
Fox Lake, IL

Over 60 years ago I defected from my country, Czechoslovakia, after the communist revolution in 1948 that forced me to live in my country. I still remember the bloody occupation by Nazi Germany in 1939 and the assassination of the ruthless protector Heydrich in 1942 for what our people paid a big prize. I was 17 years old when the gestapo arrested me in my town and put me in one notorious prison where I was interrogated and beaten up to find out where my brother was, who defected our country in 1939 to England, through many countries. They are stories that are hard to forget that sustain in my memory after so many years and I try to express my feelings for our soldiers who fought thousands of miles over the ocean for the freedom of others and the freedom for us.

Eva Claire

She has been a member of the same church for 56 years…

Kind, patient, and always available to talk about your fears…

She does know exactly how you feel, as she has buried her husband, and all 3 sons, and has also, from time to time, missed many a meal…

Sometimes she wonders, why she is still here, 84 years wise, but feeble and frail…

Clearly she is one of God's prayer warriors, while still on earth is actually quite strong…

Always a Christian, a mother, a grandmother, and a best friend, to anyone who can, with needs, fill her arms that long…

To comfort, and console, with God's guidance so sweet…

Until the Lord takes her home for her precious soul to keep…

Jeanne Freeman
High Point, NC

As I May

Match my step as we go along.
Match my mind, hum a song.
Sway with me, stay strong.
Bear with me, it won't be long.
Bide with me along the way.
Bide, through the day;
Listen to me, as I say
"Let me love you, as I may."
Match me, as I do you
Watch, as I try to do
The only thing I can for you;
To love, as I may, as true.
I'll bide with you all the way.
Until you tell me not to stay.
I'll listen to you and what you say.
"Let me love you, as I may."

Olivia Blanck
Luenburg, MA

Our 60th Wedding Anniversary

We married in our teens
People said it would not last
Our true love could not be seen.

We were blessed with a son, Paul
He will be forever our pride and joy

A tall man indeed
He is always there for us
in times of need.

Jerry I will always "love you"
You are a good man
With a sense of humor
that will be with me forever
Our vows which we took
"Til death do us part"
Were meant from our hearts

Rita Proulx
Lowell, MA

The Substitute Self

I hid myself in a tower and sent a substitute
Who would do everything that they expected,
  Until habit had made the tower a prison,
  And in terror I struggled to be free.

  Imagining freedom, I masqueraded
  In a cloak of icy indifference
And would do nothing that they expected,
Unit habit had made a new kind of prison,
  And in weakness I wept to be free.

Weeping, I beat my fists upon locked doors
  And pounded at barred windows
  Seeking my freedom all to no avail,
Until in love I found the courage to be real
  And then I knew love was the key.

Marilyn D. Aberle
Portland, OR

Snowflakes

Snowflakes fall softly.
Near the beautiful pine trees.
Out of the light blue sky.
With all different kinds of designs.
Flakes of white frosted raindrops.
Little snowflakes fall so quietly that no one can hear them.
A snowflake is as white as the clouds.
Kind of melting slowly
Everything is covered with a beautiful white blanket of snow.
Snowflakes are unique and beautiful to nature.

Zoe Bower
Lock Haven, PA

Thankful

This life I thought I didn't want
Has shown me so much
It has been incredible to be here and have a family to love
This life I wanted to give up on
Has given me a reason to live for
It has taught me I'm not alone
And to never give up on what you believe in
This life I thought I wanted to disappear
Has shown me love but also fear
I'm thankful for this life I have
And I'm thankful that I'm still here.

Kelly Salazar
Streamwood, IL

Sister to Sister

Well, Sis, let me tell you
life for me hasn't been a growing garden
they had thorns
dying plants
and places with no flowers
empty
But I've been growing
and watering
and planting seeds
sometimes digging
so Sis don't be scared
cause it's hard sometimes
but don't give up
I'm still planting
But life for me hasn't been a growing garden

Erika Hernandez
Antioch, CA

Still Life

It is about waiting for shapes to be born from emptiness
about one moment frozen in paint
it is about the time it took to make it come alive with light
yet it is anything but still,
it is about the eye sweeping the canvas
slowly, then quickly, in perfect rhythm
how forms balance and sway
like seasons, like tides in the sea
how the painter's vision changes with time
it is everything about the objects, yet nothing about them
it is about immortality and leaving thumbprints in the world
it is about our stuff, our human things:
flowers fruit
grapes wine
it is beauty in the mundane, unveiled
both timeless and finite
it is life,
still

Susan Hackel
New Milford, CT

To Natalie, on Her Thirteenth Birthday

Natalie is special for so many reasons
Whenever I see her, I think of the seasons
She's wildflowers in summer, carefree and bright
A crackling fire on a crisp, autumn night
She's refreshing and sparkling as new fallen snow
When she smiles, I see spring in her sweet, youthful glow

Like the seasons, she's changing, but one thing is sure
Her poise and grace will always endure
She's into fashion as are all of her peers
But Natalie's style will remain through the years
She's pretty, she's charming, and what sets her apart
It's not superficial, it comes from her heart

As Natalie celebrates her birthday each year
She won't just be older, she'll be all the more dear

Bonnie J. Kennelly
Cold Spring, KY

Untitled

Dappled light
Soft and yellow
Filters through a door
Left slightly ajar
Standing guard around her
While she sleeps.

Alma Graziano
Woodstock, NY

The Sweet Little Kitten

The sweet little Kitten
Had nowhere to go,
He did not have a home,
And he was knee deep in snow.

The sweet little Kitten
Had then stepped on a rock,
I saw him on the street curb;
And now his name is Brock.

The rock that Brock had stepped on,
Got kicked into the street,
It got ran over by a car,
It's nowhere to be seen.

Veronica Crawley
Bolingbrook, IL

The Giraffe's Complaint

Life may not be so very fair.
I have no home for a year.

Dogs chew and bury their bones.
They sleep in comfortable homes.

Horses eat hay off the table.
They snore loudly in the stable.

Pigs oink at the clucking hens.
They roll in mud in the pens.

Birds chirp and eat flying pest.
They sleep in a cozy, grassy nest.

Turtles swim until they're weary.
They hide in homes they carry.

Alligators swim in water waiting for meat.
They sleep where the water isn't deep.

Wallaby sitting on a couch.
With baby wallaby in her pouch.

Opossums are having an afternoon tea.
They sleep hanging upside down in the tree.

Frogs leap across the green lawn.
They nap in the lily pond.

With long legs and a long neck so plain,
Is why no one ever hears me complain!

Joyce Hew
Montebello, CA

Change

the wind whistled to me
calling me through my window screen
begging me to come away with her and dance free
under the stars and the moon
I move from my bed and stand at the window
the warm breeze softly kissing my cheeks
it reminds me of how you use to stand at my window
reaching in with your hands
to brush the hair away from my eyes
running your fingertips along the side of my face
tracing the outline of my cheek
so innocent and sweet
but now as I stand by the window
the wind slowly lets go of my hand
she understands that you are gone
and without you
I am no longer the same

Rose Schneider
Stevens Point, WI

The Moment

At this time, the world's economy is in a tailspin.
Many people couldn't wait for Obama to get in.
It was once just the "Have Nots," but now it's all classes—
The "high," as well as the "low,"
They're all wondering about how to get the dough.

Why do we try to live in the future
And miss the joy of living in the "now,"
Oftentimes questioning and worrying about the "How?"
Why try to live beyond the moment,
Which causes us so much torment;
When all we have is the moment?

Let us learn to love and live one day at a time;
Though in our pockets we may have only a dime,
And feel that our lives are in such an awful bind.
Trust God for the moment and never doubt in your mind,
He is the Giver of every day—one moment at a time.

Lula B. Moore
Greenwood, MS

Senses Lost

"The Scented Spiel reeled me unreal
and found my Senses lost."
Without my sight and without my touch
The ground hath turned to frost
And without my words my mute mouth sought
No longer do I get my point across
I hear no words I think no thoughts
Now that my Sense is lost.

Lee Beckwith
Queensbury, NY

A New Beginning

Another year is gone and passed,
The memories of joy and sorrow will last.
To some old friends, we did bid adieu,
We welcomed a new life that is brand new.
This is the start of the year ahead,
Face it with prayer and hope, embed.
We put behind us a year of trying sequences,
Now is the time to change those circumstances.
We try so hard to do our best,
Do as much as you can, to God, leave the rest.
Planning for the future will help you thrive,
Be sure to keep your dreams alive.
Keep God in your life forever entwined,
For this is a new year, your life to redesign.

Eleanore A. Wojtak
Sun City, AZ

Therapeutically in Love

When does love become Need or Need become Love?
Do we Need because we Love
Or do we Love because we Need?

Are they so closely meshed that they are one and the same,
Or are they adversaries that smother each other playing the game?
Does one prescribe one for the other in whatever degree or dosage
One perceives as his or her requirement Therapeutically?

Or is it something that we have no control over,
That is by nature and Nature's God destined to happen unplanned
And cannot be controlled or mapped to occur
Only when we want it, the way we want it?

Charles N. Joyner
Durham, NC

The Old Oak Tree

I still remember the old oak tree,
I wonder how old, that tree must be.

It was there, when I was small,
That big old tree, so round and tall.

I used to think, it would reach the sky,
In the summer heat. Under its shade, I'd lie.

The squirrels used it for nest and play,
Up and down, they'd run all day.

The birds sang, high in the top.
Each one had their favorite spot.

On its branch was a swing made from an old tire,
There I would swing, going higher and higher.

I would play in her leaves,
That fell in the fall,
Knowing before long, winter would call.

But just as it had for so many years,
Each spring it returns,
The old tree so dear.

I hope it stands there, long after I'm gone,
For my kids and grandkids to see.

I can almost hear them say,
I wonder how old that tree must be.

Betty B. Johnson
Statesville, NC

I was born in a small town called Olin. It is in Iredell County, North Carolina. This poem is about a huge oak tree that my brother and I used to play under as children. It's still there and the old house where I was raised is also there. There are still many memories that remain such as grapevines, roses and many flowers that my mother planted many years ago. I am in my sixties and love to write about many different subjects. I give copies to my church, garden club, and friends. I love poetry very much.

My Room

Listen to the rain, and don't forget the wind;
listen how it's busting through the aging windows.
I've seen this day before; it's burrowed under my skin;
I recall it in a dream that keeps recurring.

So wait, I separate, the paint on the walls drip upwards toward the
ceiling,
but I am down here, where it's plain, where the days seem more and
more like the same.

I cannot contemplate, nor conjure in;
what is beginning to seem overwhelming.
I could not forget the past, well how could it last;
I am sliding down a glass wall, there is nothing to grasp.

Just sitting in my room, for twenty years,
that held all my dreams, wishes, hope, depression, anger, fear, and tears.

Ryan Haile
Euclid, OH

I am 24 years old. I was born in Rhode Island and I recently moved to Ohio. I have a
very close knit family, but as a child I was very introverted. I isolated myself in my room
a majority of the time which inspired me to write this poem. It explains stages of my
depression and how I felt blocked from the outside world; like I was in a contained glass
box looking out. It holds a lot of my past and is a deep part of me that I'll keep inside
forever.

Untitled

Once there was a girl sitting alone wondering
when her miracle would come. Challenges, situations
all around, she felt like she was tied and bound.
Thoughts of plans filled her mind of what life
would be like if she wasn't around or maybe
in a different life, wondering what her life would
be like. The only way she could ever be
free is when she closed her eyes and lived
in her fantasies. Making different decisions,
turning back the hands of time. Also, she knew
that her life is at present time. Being a woman,
a mother, a sister and friend. Having people
to depend on her thru thick and thin. She
decided to say a prayer to reach the Man above.
Regardless of her decisions and actions of
life, she knew He had her back thru the fight.
The girl started a prayer, cried and shouted.
Pleading with the Lord, to help do something about
it. Afterwards, she felt so free cause at the
end of the day she was grateful to be here. So
whenever she gets out of spirit she pulls out
this poem and be thankful for what she has that she didn't before.

Angela Williams
NC

Love's Mistake

What would you say if our eyes met
Now somewhere down the line
Would you forgive and then forget
And say you're simply fine

How would you act should that day come
For somehow my doubts rise
Would you still smile or walk away
Or bury me with lies

Who would you blame if our words clashed
Yes sometimes tears collide
Would you think twice and bless my name
And pull me to your side

Where would your turn should time turn back
To someplace in a dream
Would you run off and wave farewell
Or vanish through the steam

Patrick Lodato
Denville, NJ

A Soft, Gentle Noise

As light as the swaying breeze
Blowing through the mystic oaks
Swirling about amidst the nighttime cloak.
A soft, gentle noise
Heard by the evening's soul.
The rushing liquid frenzy
as flows the wild stream
to the distant waterfall
vague as a forgotten dream.
A soft, gentle noise
alone in the jungle.
Light footsteps, bound and determined
moving along in the dark,
ignite the fearless spark.
A soft, gentle noise
will flicker and fade to nothing more.
The song of imaginary birds
carries for thousands of miles
They expect no reply, just
sit and listen a while.
A soft, gentle noise,
to fill a sad face with smiles.
A soft, gentle noise,
Heard forever by the evening's soul.

Jamie L. Ford
Wautoma, WI

I Stubbed My Toe on the Moon

A note of love that fluttered by
Borne away by the wind so soon
How could one ever know that I
Would stub my toe on the moon?

A warm caress and tender lips
Familiar as two lovers spoon
My young heart turned happy flips
And I stubbed my toe on the moon.

Dreams of the future seemed so real
Promises sweet as an organ tune
For me the bells would surely peal
But I stubbed my toe on the moon.

Suddenly gone is the love I seek
Lost as petals on a pathway strewn
My heart no more can think or speak
I stubbed my toe on the moon.

Marian L. Levasseur
S. Royalton, VT

My Misses

My misses she is quite a gal,
She really is my real swell pal.
Now neither, her or me are very small;
But my sweet wife is not very tall,
So the day that the mouse got in our cabin you see;
Was the day that my wife learned to fly; at least it seemed that way to me.
Now out by the kitchen table, where all the chairs are aligned;
She jumped to the top of a chair and landed on her feet and not her behind.
It was only a little mouse, grey as could be;
But to the size of that mouse we could never agree.
This was the woman who faced 27 kids each day;
Who was always teaching them and in on their play.
Well, me, the big hero, the man of the house,
Just happened to be there to finish off the mouse.
Now, I have killed deer and bear; that was sure a lot bigger and more of a deal;
But slaying the mouse that day for my wife was really the best kill.
Now as the winter drags on and she forgets that day;
Do you think it would be wrong to bring another mouse into play?
'Cause, boy, it's a good living to have a wife love you so;
Who looks up to you as a hero, you know?
Boy! I am glad the cat didn't get the first
When I saw them in the barn and I am kinda ashamed, the idea was the worse;
But believe me, I will never tell her and that is for sure;
I don't know if she knew it, if our marriage would endure.

Country Tom Bowser
Nixa, MO

Howdy! I'm Country Tom Bowser and I live in the wonderful USA in beautiful Ozarks. Janice, my wife, and I love our retired life in our log home 100 feet from the James River's edge. We enjoy our 2 dogs, 2 horses, and other critters that come around. We have 6 children: Tim, Ted, Tod, Tammy, Tommy and Tyler plus grandchildren and great-grandchildren scattered from Florida to Alaska. This 73-year-old cowboy now teaches horseback riding. The love of family, friends, and "pets" has given me reason to enjoy my gift of writing cowboy poetry over the years.

First Meeting

Come into the stall slowly.
A scared colt will KNOW your apprehension...
Breathe deeply, exhale, relax.

Know in every moment his fear grows
your danger is heightened.
Do not crowd him, yet speak softly,
perhaps telling of a time
when you too were afraid.

Now kneel,
let him take the first step.

Patience,
his trust is worth waiting for.
With ears held forward
and eyes showing white,
he will approach,
extending his soft muzzle
to find and know your scent.

Inhale his breath
then blow it gently back into nostrils,
for an instant,
breathe as one...

Amye K. Lilienthal
Dannebrog, NE

Marriage

How unique!
To find two people, who become one,
Learning to be friends at first,
Who are different in many ways,
Molding, and bending, to blend into one,
Until, one day their friendship turns to love.
You are each others best friend,
You can't wait to be with the other,
At the end of the day,
Catching up on each day's adventures,
Missing each other when your apart,
The feeling of being half, of who you really are.
Two halves, who make a whole,
That's the way it should be,
Two become as one,
Taking care of each others needs.
Feeling safe with the other,
Walking into old age together,
What adventures you have seen,
In all the years in between.
Marriage, there is no love like it,
It's what life is all about,
"Thank God," for sending you your "soulmate."

Elizabeth Dold
Bunnell, FL

A Lifetime Crush

My heart undergoes palpitations each time he enters the room
My breathing increases ever so slightly
My hands begin to tremble ever so slightly
It's still hard for my eyes to meet his...

No one must know...
I lower my head ever so slightly
As I smile to myself (He is mine)
I can feel my foot tapping ever so slightly
When I hear his voice
I'm trying not to become fidgety
I know that he is coming my way

No one knows
Why after all of this time I still feel giddy?
I get giddy when he goes grocery shopping
When he cooks dinner after a long day at work

No one must know...
But I still get giddy when he washes the clothes
And plays basketball with our daughter

No one knows...

That the man that makes me giddy...still
Is my best friend, my soulmate, my soulja
My Husband
My lifelong CRUSH...

Julia St. George
Turnersville, NJ

I am the mother of an amazing 14-year-old daughter, Chloe, and the wife of a remarkable man, Keith. Keith and I have been married for twenty years and he is the inspiration for this poem. He continues to put Chloe and me first in his life. It is with pride that I devote this poem to him. YBLMA because IALY.

First Love Lost

I have to go, my darling
I really don't have a choice
But he couldn't really hear
The quivering in her voice

She didn't really know what
She would do with out him by her side
And he would never really know
How many days that she had cried

She knew that she would love him forever
But she knew that she had to try
To live the life that they had planned
The time was short before he died

She remembered the day they met
And how it was so long ago
But he was really the right one
And she never wanted to let him go

She'll never feel his arms hold her
So long and strong
She'll never have his broad shoulder
To cry on when she's wrong

And when her heart finally mends
And a new love she has found
She'll take him to the graveyard
To meet her first love in the ground

Bari L. Schwickerath
Sandwich, IL

Soldier of Soldiers

Standing strong, holding tight, a soldier of soldiers, with the will to
  fight.
We battle the bills, to manage the house, to keep the kids from running
  out.
We have grey hairs by the time we're 30 but we're the soldier of
  soldiers standing sturdy.
So 30 is here, we are losing our minds and the prices go up on the
  things we buy, the car breaks down and now we're like Fred.
But hey, the soldier of soldiers are moving ahead.
Now 40 has turned the corner, and we've made it to the top, we paid
  the bills on time and had to stop.
So a new job is found, and he makes a career.
My soldier of soldiers without any fear.
So 50 will reach us.
Our marriage would have been long, I'll love him more then, than ever
  before.
Our friends and our families and all those we love, are the ones that
  make us the soldiers we've become.

Elishia Lough
Greenwood, IN

A Box of Bite Size Doughnut Holes

Would you light my cigarette in the wind for me,
My sweet lipped blue-eyed girl of fun?
Come take my hand and I will invite you in,
To my playhouse beyond the sun!
In the kitchen of my playhouse made of tin,
A young witch sits with apron strings undone.
And upon the shelf waits a box of bite-sized doughnut holes,
Enough for everyone!
A cluster of diamonds, a string of pearls,
Shine like bright candles on my misery.
While fingers point at me by snickering girls,
Asking what poor man is he?
Blue ribbons adorn the silver of our fine tablefare,
At the place where we eat.
Like the pearly white beads that grace the belly of a whore,
Who once chose to kiss me there so sweet!
Apples on the table, peaches on the shelf, pie cherry's in the bowl,
But nothing can compare ever sweeter by themselves,
Quite like those bite-sized doughnut holes!

Mark R. Wettstein
Millville, NJ

ATribute to My Sister

Nine months have passed since that sad day
The one we loved was called away
The call was sudden, the shock severe,
With little thought that death was near.

Only those who have lost can tell the pain
But in my memory you still remain.
Friends may think I have forgotten
When at times they see me smile
Little do they know the heartache
That lingers all the while.

To your grave I wander
The flowers I place with care
No one knows the heartache
As I turn and leave you there.

Time goes by but memories stay
As dear and near as yesterday
But in my heart you are with me yet
I love you too much to ever forget…

Betty Reid
Sylva, NC

Goodbye, You!

I live in the dark where it is always blue.
I live in fear because of you.
Shame, guilt, bruises, I dare not tell.
No one knows because I hide it so well.
You promised to love me "till death do us part."
Slowly but surely, you have broken my heart.
Where did I go so wrong? What did I do?
To receive such pain and hatred from you.
You mean the world to me, the man I got to know.
Where is he? Tell me, where did he go?
I'm sorry for your past or whatever makes you mad.
I just want you to be a good husband and an even better dad.
The kids and I are leaving, but know that I will pray for you at night.
For you're the father of my children so I hope you will be alright.
No more dark.
No more blue.
No more fear.
Good Bye, You!

Krissy Jones Henry
Wellston, OH

Britty Is a Proper Cocker

Britty is a proper cocker
She's a dog, a cocker spaniel of black and white.
She's always nice to everyone she never wants to fight

Britty is a proper cocker
She always follows the golden rule
No matter where she is, a store, at home or school

Britty is a proper cocker
She always tries to give her help to anyone she saw
She's there at every turn to lend a helping paw

Britty is a proper cocker
Instead of saying "I didn't do it, it wasn't me!"
She's always first to say "I'm sorry."

Britty is a proper cocker
She doesn't need to beg on bended knees
All she does is smile so sweetly and just say "Please."

Britty is a proper cocker
She received a gift from someone that she knew
She told her friend very sincerely "Thank You!"

Britty is a proper cocker
She knows it feels good to be clean and neat
She always looks marvelous to everyone she meets.

Yes, Britty is a proper cocker

Susan McNamara
Trenton, MI

Twins and Heroes

The twins stood tall and proud
reaching for the sky
Then evil reared its ugly head
and left us all to cry
As quick as a bolt of lightning
our lives were turned around
We didn't want to believe our eyes
or listen to the sound
Then came the many heroes
afraid but oh so brave
They put their fears behind them
and looked for those to save
Loved ones sit in silence
not sure what they will hear
Some praying to their God above
to spare the ones held dear
The heroes keep on searching
exhausted they may be
But something tells them not to quit
and they go back to see
Lady Liberty is once again
the landmark we so love
And one day there will be new twins
reaching high above

Joan R. Smith
Harper Woods, MI

Shampoo

There are different types of shampoos
One is only best
The best is the bad
The good is the most best
I only use one kind
That kind is the best
I know so
I am an expert
The experts know the best of the best
The shampoo is the cleanest kind
It makes my hair so clean
The shampoo is the shiniest
It looks so bright and colorful
It makes me happy and joyful

Elizabeth Maxwell
Neeses, SC

I've Lost My Watch

Oh me! Oh my!
I've lost my watch and I could cry.
For how am I going to be late
Without a watch to tell me so?

And, if perhaps, I accidentally
Be on time,
Will this not upset the natural order
Of the universe?

Mother Nature, I've been told
Does not like to be fooled.
I'm quite sure that Father Time
Is not one with whom to trifle.

Oh me! Oh my!
Without my watch how will I know
When it is my time to die?
I had so planned on being late and missing that!

Karolyn Bowen
White River Junction, VT

The Dream

I dream I walked the desert
In a blood-orange evening sky
And I heard the call to prayer
From a minaret nearby
So I laid a branch of olive
In the mosque's open door
And I heard a voice call "sister"
As I knelt upon the floor.

Then I dreamed I saw a temple
In Jerusalem the Fair
And the singing of the cantor
Was a poem on the air
And the olive branch I carried
Rustled softly as I stood
And a sign read "All are welcome here
Who come in brotherhood."

Then I dreamed a great cathedral
Stood amid a city street
With its portal worn to smoothness
By the fall of many feet
And I took a branch of olive
And I stepped inside to pray,
And a voice said "We will all
Pray with one voice, one heart, one day."

Nancy Sheridan
Lexington, VA

Two Flowers

I used to be a flower
A long, long time ago.
But those who had the power
To help me thrive and grow
Had more important things to do
Than cater to my needs.
They watched their flower slowly shrink
Into a pile of weeds.

My mother was a flower, too.
But not like me at all.
Her presence so commanding that
A giant would look small
Beside a centerpiece so grand.
For all the world to see.
It isn't hard to understand
Why no one noticed me.

Majestic, regal, like a queen
Who would not leave her throne.
Not heeding those insisting that
Her glory was all gone.

But they were right, and I was wrong.
And now I can't pretend.
The flower I could not emulate
Will never bloom again.

Barbara Nathan
Bronx, NY

As the daughter of two teachers, a love for writing was instilled in me from an early age. I was eight years old when I started writing poetry. I am a native of New York. I have a Master's degree in psychology and am a retired social worker. I wrote this poem in 2006 shortly after my mother quietly succumbed, after a thirteen-year struggle with Alzheimer's Disease, one week before her ninety-third birthday. Visiting her every month in her Florida Nursing home did not lessen my difficulty accepting the changes in her. Writing this poem helped me heal.

You Are Invited

It doesn't matter what you've done,
Or even who you know.
Nor does it matter who you are,
We've all been invited to go.
The invitations were sent to us
Many long years ago...
There's going to be a celebration,
The Bible tells us so.
The invitation says,
"My children, come unto Me,
We'll have a wedding feast...
This is where I want you to be,
I wait with outstretched arms,
But you must send back your reply.
The time is running out...
You must answer before you die.
When your reply is received,
Your name will be written down,
Then as you enter the gate...
I'll give to you a crown.
You'll never more know death and pain,
There'll be no more tears or strife,
All because your name is written
In the Lamb's great book of life."

Retta A. Miller
Punxsutawney, PA

A Seagull's Flight

A seagull flying
In the rain,

Lands and perches
On a toll poll,

Standing still
Saluting the
Long awaited
Rain,

Soaking up the
Showers of
Blessings from
On high,

Under accumulated
Clouds; from our
Oh, most high,

"Oh, that man would
Praise the Lord for
His wonderful works."

Amen

Delores A. Cohens
Greenville, SC

Take Time

Dishes to wash, clothes to dry
Take time out to bake a pie.

Vacuum the rug, dust furniture, too
Take time out to make a stew.

Change the sheets, iron the shirts
Take time out, dad goes to work.

Clean the house, put children to bed
Take time out to straighten my head.

Peace at last, but before the day ends
Take time out to visit with friends.

Judith A. Bossarte
Van Burren, AR

The Deed

Once in a moment all caution dismiss
With reality but a dream
The deed we shared in that night of bliss
Will one day rise to scream
And wither the lips of a lover's kiss
In the light of truths bright gleam
And carry away the things we'll miss
In penitence bitter stream

Andrew W. Van Houten
Columbus, OH

Miles and Years

You are being mistreated
Your heart aches with tears
You need to get away
In miles and years
Miles will put distance between,
You and whoever is treating you mean
Years will pass and time will tell,
How much better you will prevail
Do not just hope that things will improve,
The best for you is to make a move
Erase all your doubts and all your fears
You need to get away
In miles and years!

Lester S. Hill
Huntington Park, CA

270

Heaven's Glory

Have you ever heard of the old, old story?
How a babe came down from Heaven's glory.

He was born of a virgin named Mary,
And it was proclaimed verily, verily.

That this babe would be,
The way of salvation for you and me.

It was in God's plan from the beginning,
To provide a perfect ending.

This tiny babe was borne,
In a stable with cows, sheep, donkeys, and corn.

When he was only twelve years old,
He went to the temple it was told.

He taught the teachers of law,
And everyone was astonished by it all.

His parents were of lowly estate,
Yet, this child would become the way to enter Heaven's Gate.

At the age of thirty his work began,
His mission ministry was at hand.

But this man was destined to die,
Because of the sin of you and I.

Linda Hill
West Plains, MO

Just Believe

Just believe in yourself,
In your feelings,
In your faith,
And in whatever you are dreaming.

Just believe in a friendship,
In a child's loving embrace,
In that special someone,
And in ones smiling face.

Just believe what's in your heart,
What's in your thoughts,
What's in your wishes,
And what's in your mind you seem to sought.

Just believe in miracles,
In hope,
In a loving glance,
And in a family unbroken circle.

Just believe in prayers,
In love,
In angels,
And in God's loving care.

Just believe in what you do and in what you want,
You can achieve it,
It can happen, if you just believe it.

Michael J. Clement
Labadieville, LA

Obstacles in Our Way

So many obstacles on my way
To your heart
To many to control
I hear you calling out my name
Pulling me closer as I go
Where are you my love?
I call out to you to help me
On the way
Wondering if we will ever find
Each other with all these
Obstacles in our way.

Krystal Felder
Sevierville, TN

Oversight

Sulfuric stench of a freshly lit match penetrates the dark
Sweet to the nose of a forgotten child
Left alone to revel in this thought of redemption
His nimble fingers pry off a rotten piece of board from the wall
Just enough air let in to let the candle breathe

The family Ford races away to discover merriment
Leaving behind the harsh reality of past endeavors
Weary eyes watch through the air passage
Looking forward to the thought of a minimal peace
And allow sleep to come to an oversight

Leah Carruth
Lubbock, TX

Blue

The sky is Blue and my face is glued to you
And sometimes I felt like you blew me away
You tried to tell me, But like the wind
I flew away when I realized
that I grew too far away from you
I blew back and drew you closer to me
Don't let the world get in the way of us,
I love you so You created me and my
Life is short and it blows away too
Fast bring me to the promised land
With honey and blueberries better than
Ever, Blue sky, Blue sky show me to
My creator For I know that you are
Behind there you will come from there

Carina Renteria
Brentwood, CA

Love's Journey

Love is a lifelong journey,
One I have chosen to make,
With you close beside me
As my partner and my mate.

Our memories, our secrets,
The ones only between us two.
Together they unite us
Until this life through.

To be without you in my life
Would be a missing part.
You have known me like no other.
You have known me from the start.

You have shared my greatest moments.
You have seen my greatest pain.
You have stood beside me quietly.
Your love has still remained.

Yes, love is a lifelong journey,
How I love you to my core,
And as the years pass by us
I grow to love you more.

Leanna Simpson
Clive, IA

Ms. Jiggy

It all began at the age of 4
Great personality, bright smile
With the knack to explore;

Had a dream to be famous
In hopes everyone would adore;

Then along came life full of adversities
No one could believe;

Out the window went my dreams
And all my self-esteem;
Started clubbing, wilding, jumping
On stage like an exotic dancer;

Little did I know men, drugs,
Alcohol was not the answer.

Was left with no hope, no desire
No trust in a person;

Searched within, found God
In the midst of my diversion.

So instead of regretting my obstacles,
Hurdles and unfortunate attacks;

I've learned to open my heart
To forgive and give back.

Jessica Polanco
Boynton Beach, FL

As a young girl I was very outgoing and full of life. I loved to sing and dance. As a result of being raised in a dysfunctional family, I developed low self-esteem and my dreams of show business eventually faded. I am currently a full-time caregiver for the elderly. Caring for the elderly was the best thing that's ever happened to me. It has taught me a lot of lessons including a lot about myself. I live by the motto, "Be the best you can be in all that you do."

Thinking Straight

I don't so much need jewels or land—
And a security system to hide me;
More than these I need a friendly hand
And one clear Star to guide me.

Oh, it's a pleasure to own a glittering stone,
And I might like a fabulous yacht;
But these would grow pale, they'd sink low in the scale
Compared to the folks I've got.

I treasure my eyes, the soft evening skies,
All the beauty of the day and the night;
But what is more is my memory's store
And a measure of inward Light.

Fame may exclude me; success can elude me;
Applause I can do without—
But, please, never let me lose this insight to choose
And a Faith that is stronger than Doubt.

Mildred H. Miles
Kingston Spring, TN

I'm an eighty-six year old widow, blind, and lame. I am thankful for all I can still do. My deceased husband was the love of my life. We raised three fine children. I taught English for 27 years and Sunday School for 68 years. I could never achieve the lyrical beauty that characterizes all good poetry, but I sometimes thought I had something worth saying. I came to know absolutely that among life's priceless treasures are things like a happy home, a sustaining faith, good friends, and a clear conscience. This knowledge was my motivation for writing "Thinking Straight."

Death of the Sinner

In the silence that remains when the mourners are gone, you are left
alone to think.
O, the morbid air that lingers on until at last your fate shall come.
But that you had taken heed!

Only now you must regret—regret forever all your wrongs.
Nothing not to do but wait, wait til the judging of your fate,
The fate you know but refuse to realize. Alone you are left, your life to
analyze.

Now, too plainly you can see, how wrong you were, how foolish your
deeds.
Alas, too late, your life is done. You plead, you beg, you sob, you
mourn,
But nevermore your chance to right your wrongs; you have wasted your
last chance.

Accept your fate, you know you must; to burn in hell for all your lust.
The wasted years and months and weeks you could have saved yourself
at least,
But now you are lost, gone forever.

Thou canst say thy God is heartless; scores of years you had to change.
Here, alone, you watch and wait—
Sorry now, but alas, too late.

Betty Roberts
Wilcox, AZ

True Friends

~The Smiles and Giggles~
The Fights and the Tears
We've stayed together
Through many years

~The inside jokes
And cute photographs
Fun memories
And lots of laughs

Funny stories
Pinky swears
Promises
And secrets shared

Other friends will come and go
But True Friends stay
Through thick and thin
~Through rain and snow~

Hannah Campbell
Weymouth, MA

By the Lake

The crickets chirp
The sun sets
On my lonely heart
In my empty bed.
The bees are busy
Pollinating flowers
I could stay here
For hours and hours.
The lake glistens
Boats ROAR,
Trees rustle,
My Father snores,
Sleep on, dear Father,
While our world changes
Outside our house by the
Lake.

Devon M. Bleyaert
Canton, MI

Beat the Clock

Time
Only a construct
Tracking change in growing things
Yet, somehow, has a spirit of its own

I beckon to it
Believing reasoning is a valid force
Pleading for some cooperation
So dependant
That when I imagine it's scarce
My own thinking makes me tense

Mixed with memory, it edits reality
And I swear it slows
With grief
And speeds with fullness,
Contrary to my expectation,
Yet I am powerless

So, I try to attend to now
To disengage
From this futile conflict
And be
Here,
In this moment,
Growing

Cindy Ostuni
Syracuse, NY

Black and White History

November 4, 2008 History was made.
September 11, 2001 in the United States of America every heartache
with pain.

Twin towers building in New York City two little girls in the White
House.
The year 2008 we need a change,
The year 2001 I don't want to remember,
But I can't forget.
History can be good and history can be sad,
I guess from both years there is something to learn.
November 4, 2008 decisions were made for you, Mr. President.
September 11, 2001 cowardly and evil decision were made to end a
chapter of history in the lives of many innocent people who did
not get the chance to see history being made on November 4, 2008.

Gladys Ponce
Waukegan, IL

Imprisoned Love

Your love is like a prison cell,
You lock me up inside your hell.
Your possessive bars upon the sill,
The ball and chain at my heel.
Domineering, is the lock and key.
The ache in my heart should I go free.

Your love is like a Dungeon Pit,
You play my mind when you see fit,
Jealousy is at the gate.

Suspiciously guarding, you lie and wait.
The skies outside are gray and black,
They match your love for me exact.
The lightning, then boom the crackling thunder,
In the light of my weaknesses you get stronger.

The tormenting hell you put me through,
The anguish I feel for loving you.
I hoped you'd change, but the same you stay.
So I must leave for strength I pray.
I must have courage, I've got to be brave,
For in leaving you, its me I save!

Joyce L. Rios
Granit City, IL

In the Tunnel of Hope

In the Tunnel of Hope
I am in the tunnel.
It is dark
My mind is not there.
I need a friend
A flower to smell
The beauty of a smiling child.
I need to dance,
to laugh, to smile
I need to look in the eyes
of someone to see love.
I need love.
Suddenly I see a light.
I am going where the light is.
I am out of the tunnel
Now I am happy because I have
Life and love.

Valeria G. Carratello
Forest Hills, NY

Osama Bin Laden

Osama Bin Laden (may his tribe decrease)
Awoke one dawn from a nightmare of peace.
He saw in candlelight within his cave
Some Taliban with bearded faces brave.

And then a hand wrote on the limestone wall
A camouflaged, uncertain, messy scrawl,
And since Osama could not read the print,
He asked, "Can you tell me what is meant?"

The hand to human form materialized;
With this response Osama was apprised:
"The names of those who kill the infidel
Intent to send these "faithless" into hell."

And is my name thereon?" Osama mused.
"Indeed it is," the wraith at once accused,
"But you assume it's Allah's message here
And that is furthest from the truth, I fear.
It is the C I A's "Most Wanted" list
And your Bin Laden name leads all the rest."

Hubert N. Whitten
Bridgewater, VA

Love, Open Arms, and Trust

I know you feel lost
That no one is there beside you anymore
They tell you to listen
But all you hear is the silence
You lost the closest thing to you
And you know it cannot be replaced
Although it is not the same person
When one is taken another is born
What you feel is unbearable
And yet hard to deal with
The feelings are like scars
     People can see them, but
Only you know the story
     Scars do fade with time
But they are put there for a reason
     The mind does forget things when it grows older
But with the scar that is left behind
     Drilled so deeply into your heart
It is just the start of showing
     Everyone how much you love them
Don't push the people away, that love you
     We can help you through anything
With open arms and hearts to fill with love
     All you have to do is believe and trust in us

Rachael Everhart
Bellefontaine, OH

Silently, I Waltz Against the Beat

Twisted are my scattered thoughts, had I perhaps stumbled upon an
unforgiving incident...
Bumping my fragile noggin', awaking to an awkwardly,
unprecedented, still blackness...
Imagine sensing oneself smothering silently, whirling in a dance of
music seldom heard...

Those mingling about are abundant, kindred passing souls stepping a
dance against the beat...
Bound, savagely clawing from within the presence of "nailed" souls...
Independently, I have, I hold collective moments, my impatient
memories of me, myself and I...

Taunts of yesterdays of who, of we; so twisted the hindrance of our
harsh reality...
Banished to begin again, to be reborn of a truly flawed presence...
Impatiently, I resist the inter dwelling of turmoil, to find acceptance in
my newly unpatterned stride...

Thought to have truly passed of existence, between living to death, I
am momentarily breathless...
Balanced precariously, between a backwards sweeping whirl and a
forward falling perseverance...
Imprisoned motionlessly, driven fluently, I protest the stance of limbo
here...

Traumatically...
Brain fully...
Injured...
I waltz silently to the dance of my own disheveled beat...

Lauri J. Gerace
Tully, NY

Hello and thank you for sharing this moment to waltz with me. Autumn born 1961, I am
an Upstate New York artist. Though I am not known for my poetry (my choice medium
of personal journaling), it was at this moment I felt driven to express myself in a public
forum. Recently having suffered a second traumatic brain injury in my life, I found the
inspiration for this collective arrangement of thoughts. I acknowledge my art of endless
mediums to be my greatest positive, healing strength. I dedicate this poem to my doctors
and grandson Ian, my firecracker of joy, who guides me through.

Yesterday's Past

It seems we're floating
Through the embers of our destiny.

What will you take from me?
When we look back upon tomorrow,
Will you remember all the fantasy.

We lived in the shadows of
The candy-coated skyscrapers that
Blocked the rays of insanity.

I loved you every day.

While memories have faded
My love never has.
It seems we're drifting now
Through the sediment of our past.

What we've built up
Can never be torn down.

Daniel J. Flosi
Glendale, AZ

On a Train Going Nowhere

There, but for a gift of fate go I, unkempt, unshaven, stretched across three seats asleep and momentarily free, only to awaken to an uncaring world from which he had escaped for a few rumbling, slumbering moments.
As his eyes opened they seemed to say, "God, why did you awaken me. Where am I going, what's around the corner for a broken heart, and empty pockets?"

Reading the faraway look in his sunken eyes, I hoped it would be a hot meal, a much needed bath, a friendly smile and a new sense of direction. But I felt in my heart that he would come to his unknown destination alone, unloved, no hope, no home, no one waiting for this lonely target of unfriendly glances.

As I got off the train at the next station, his eyes were closing again, probably an effort to lock out the gaze of the so-called affluent world. I paused a moment on the platform, watching the snake-like means of transportation rolling into the emptiness that awaited this lonely creature on a down-bound train going nowhere.

Going up the stairs into the great metropolis of eight million people, I hoped he would someday soon catch an up-town express to the Great American Dream.

Barney Mulligan
Pearl River, NY

From Awe to Awful

When did I lose my desire to romp and play outside?
When did I lose my love for the winter season?
When did I lose the child within?
When did I lose my feelings of awe when viewing the fallen snow?
When did the awe become irritation, concern and fatigue?

When the snow continued to fall every few days and was blanketed by a layer of ice.
When falls and breaks became a major safety concern.
When my XCountry skis remained in storage.
When my miniature dachshund cried upon her walk.
When the forecast became more snow, ice and rain.
When feelings of isolation became paramount.

How do I find my childlike "awe" buried deep within myself as the snow and ice continue to bury the ground?

Sonya McCubrey
Wethersfield, CT

My Country

I'm Thankful for my eyes to see
This Promise Land Thou has given me.

I'm Thankful for my hands to feel
The good brown earth that will plenty yield.

I'm Thankful for my feet to trod
Through the green pastures and Golden Rod.

I'm Thankful for my ears to hear
The Meadow Lark's little song of cheer.

I'm Thankful for my body, strong,
A voice that I can raise in song.

I'm Thankful, Oh my Lord to Thee,
That I was born in this Country...Free!

June D. Penleton
Ogden, UT

I Am That Breeze

I whistle like the wind.
I am everywhere…and nowhere.
Feel me on your face,
As I flow through your hair.
I am that breeze.

I have my spouts, yes.
Tornadoes rise from my tantrums
And hurricanes from my sadness.
Though do not expect this from me,
For I am almost never like this.
Usually I am a warm wind that dances through the trees.
I am that breeze.

A deep desire to be free, yes, that is me.
I play with your passion,
And sing to your heart.
But your soul is what I truly satisfy.
For only I, in a brief and fleeting moment, am magic.
Enjoy me while you can because soon,
I will blow another way.
I am that breeze.

Jamie Perry
Palatine, IL

The Presentation

There is a pain in my world like no other
I can't tell you, you wouldn't understand
You'd think much different of what I thought
But now, I believe this pain should be banned

It upsets me more than one may think
It brings stormy clouds into my world
I am looking for this odd missing link
I'm mad, and frustrated, and sad just as well

This pain makes me wonder
Why people judge the way they do
I hear the booming thunder
And think; what she says isn't true

God has given me a way to fight back
Yeah I could scream, and I could yell
But I've got something that this person lacks
I've got dignity, pride…and truth just as well

Stacie Dahlbeck
Lubbock, TX

I Wish I Had an Elephant

I wish I had an elephant
He'd be big and tall.
He'd bring me to school each day
And all I'd have to do is call.

I wish I had a chipmunk
To dig beneath the ground.
We'd dig a hole to China
To see what could be found

I wish I had a zebra
To frolic in the street.
We'd play tricks on all the neighbors
And we' enjoy hide and seek.

I wish I had these animals
But, alas, I can have none.
My dad is terribly allergic
Which takes away all the fun.

Daniell Klosowski
Schaumburg, IL

The Poet Within Us All

Thoughts trickling through
    Over and over
A dripping faucet
    The tune plays incessantly
    In my head
Till alas the plumber arrives
    As the pen takes to paper
Or is it…
    Brush to canvas
    Lens to photoshoot
    Clay to sculpture
    Choreography to dance
    Notes to symphony
Oh the endless expressions
How will your geyser
    Spew forth
    As it breaks ground?

Mary Baribeau
Pacific Grove, CA

The Rosary Vs. Shock and Awe

While saying my daily rosary,
Outside my daughter's home in Medford,
A "screaming" jet flying overhead,
Disturbed the tranquil peace of the day,
With the worse-sounding noise I've ever heard,

I thought of "shock and awe" and Bush's war—
How awful it came to be, only death and destruction it ultimately
  bore,

The rosary says prayers for peace on earth,
And "shock and awe" destroys it all,
No more joy, and no more mirth,
A man who thought he was almighty king,
Brought the world misery, no peace did he bring,

It came at a horrific price, our sons and daughters
Lost their precious lives.

He wants victory at any cost saying he is our commander-in-chief,
Our only true and deserving boss.

It is sad, indeed, that our voices are made mute,
Only Bush creates his vision that no one is able to refute.

But, still I pray my rosary each and every day for lasting peace.
That this nasty beast, "shock and awe," will finally cease.

Lori Stotlar
Milpitas, CA

The Sea's Rhythmic Lullaby

I hear the roaring waves, I feel foamy water against my feet; the wind is blowing my hair in all directions,

The wind is untamable; it is wild and free; blowing wherever it pleases;

The wind has a salty smell like the sea; the sand is sinking beneath my feet the sand is not coarse, but smooth and soft;

as I look behind me I gaze at my footprints on this beach the evidence being washed away everyday;

I stop to pick up a shell; I know that it once was a hermit crab's home but now it is vacant; I toss it into the sea; and I watch as the sea engulfs it and it disappears into the depths;

The water is roaring loudly and the waves are crashing against the rocks but with all this sound and noise I feel very peaceful and quiet; the waves are like a rhythmic lullaby that makes you want to rest and sleep;

I stoop down and pick up a stick that is by my feet I take it up and throw it into the water and watch as the waves carry it out to sea;

I find a large boulder to sit on by the water and I watch the sun set on the horizon; I begin to walk back to the house leaving only my footprints behind.

Brently L. Pennington
Amarillo, TX

Old Man

Old man sittin' on the side of the road
A brown bottle in his hand,
Tellin' his stories of the Golden Days
When he was a younger man.

You see the years have caught up to him
In a short matter of time.
The calloused hands and the worn out shoes
They seem to suit him fine.

Old man can I walk with you for just another mile.
Old man can I talk with you for just a little while.

We sat and talked awhile about life out on the road,
The darkened alleys that we layed our heads
And the nights out in the cold.
When he talked it was like a song playin' on my radio
He was tellin' of his long lived years
And how he lost his soul.

He told me about the things he's done
And the places he has been.
He told me that he had his bottle and that was his only friend.

So Old Man can I walk with you for just another mile.
Old man can I talk with you for just a little while.

Jeffrey Andrus
Bath, NY

I'm forty-eight years old. I live in a small town in western New York. I've been writing over twenty years. I play guitar and drums. I've written two children's stories, many songs, and a lot of poetry. What inspired this poem was the homeless problem. If people would take the time to talk to these forgotten souls, they'd realize they're humans too. They all have stories of their own and hence, "Old Man." After talking to him, I was compelled to write these lines. I hope you enjoy it.

298

A Grandmother's Rights

Gone are my rights I promised my daughter
The day she died to keep my grandsons safe.

I did my best for seven long years while my daughter lived with us, and
the grandchildren were left in my care long afterwards.

Now the system says no, I can't be in contact except by phone because
of someone's past,
it's not right to this person,
and myself who helped take the boys to the doctor,
made things for them to eat,
put a roof over their heads,
let them build things with their own two hands,
were there for them when their dad beat them,
and wouldn't stand the sight of them.

Our love we gave these little boys,
So I say the system may take my grandsons away,
Even though they want to live with us,
But my love,
The rest of my family,
My son, their uncle, included,
Will never even and I know will certainly not be diminished in their
hearts,
but in the end, I guess I did keep my promise.

Jan E. Lanham
Kincaid, WV

Eight to Ten

I'm not looking for a gold band
Under somebody's hand
Being a man's number one fan

I'm looking for a man worth eight to ten years

Some men I can take for eight to ten months
Most wear me out in eight to ten weeks
Some have a shelf life of eight to ten days

To spend eight to ten hours with some would get me
Eight to ten years.

Rose O'Callaghan
Glens Falls, NY

Untitled

One year has now passed since you've been gone
Now just a memory from dusk till dawn.
Sunshine today doesn't sound too bad
Some called him Ray and I called him Dad.
When faced with a problem you always cared
Good times and humor were things that you shared.
Your favorite number was lucky seven
A wonderful friend now living in Heaven.
Our lives with you, a pleasure we've met
One excellent father we will never forget!

Carl Kowalski
Alpena, MI

All That He Took

All that he took was the spirit of my soul and the freedom to live.
All that he took was my ability to reason what I used to understand.
He took the ability for me to walk again.
He took my heart with him after he broke it into a million pieces.
He even took my individuality, the parts that make me unique and
special in every way, that part that makes me myself.
All that he took was my trust and devotion when he abused me
physically and verbally.
All that he took were my eyes, by punching them so hard that they
ended up being bruised and I ended up being blind.
However, I cannot distinguish why someone I fell in love with and
thought the whole world of would do something so horrible to me.
After all he has done, you would think he'd learn, no not him, he just
repeatedly does the same thing over and over again.
You ask, "Why am I still with a deceitful man?" It's because my love
for him ever since we were married was everlasting. Can't you see?
Even if I stay in the same situation that I am in, I might get more
beatings and end up dead.
Now that I realize what I must do to get out of this abusive relationship,
I am willing to finally get out. But I cannot, because he already
took my life with a gun.
I am at a better place now called Heaven. Here I can finally be free.

Brittany DeGagne
Fall River, MA

301

Memories I Keep

Tucked away in my underwear drawer
These are the things that I adore.
A belt from my mother's house dress;
A handkerchief ah;
Two—One of my father's and one of my husband's;
Nestled together among my mess.
Such good memories never forgotten.
Makes tears come to my eyes about all these guys.
I miss them.
They're all up in Heaven having a ball;
My husband, my father, my mother—all—
Every once in a while I'll straighten this out.
That's how this poem came all about.
Not to forget our other family members.
Dear Rita and Bill and Stew
They're up there and missed and loved
    and tears are shed for them too.

Jean Haughn
Muncie, IN

Eleven September

Eleven September, year two thousand one
A day like no other whose dawn had begun.
Clear, bright and sunny, who could foretell
Before it was over, those visions of hell.

All boarded the jets for a routine air flight.
Only nineteen knew they would never see night.
Their God and Jihad to them only mattered,
By these few alone the peace would be shattered.

Helped by the surprise, they took over each plane,
The passengers thinking they were quite insane.
This struggle complete, the now weapons turned east,
On course for the targets New York and D.C.

In the big city the Trade Center looming
With work underway and janitors grooming.
The Pentagon in the District was humming.
A field in Penn state knew not what was coming.

The first missile crashed in a huge ball of flame,
With everyone watching the second one came.
In the five-sided building a fire was lit,
While heroes aborted the fourth scheduled hit.

Gasping in horror as twin towers crumbled,
In sorrow and confusion all felt humbled.
September eleven, make ready the bell
For those who remain, may they sound the death knell.

Mark C. Beil
Wauwatosa, WI

A Day in the Life

I woke this morning early no longer can I sleep,
The first day on my new job, excitements running deep.
Gone are the cutesy dresses and the fancy little shoes,
My new outfit is permanent—called California blues.
I step into my uniform, pressed, crisp, and new.
Instantly I'm taller, stronger, badder too.
Gone is the little cutie that everyone adores
Now I bring down bad guys, druggies, thieves and whores.
I am a police officer, my shield I wear with pride.
I feel amazingly capable with confidence I can't hide.
There's no place I'm afraid to go, my gun strapped to my side.
Make no mistake it's by the book, no rookie moves for me.
My backup piece I keep close by, where none will ever see.
I'm very thankful for this job, to protect and serve,
So please do not mistake this face; it's backed by lots of nerve.
Now do not make me shoot you, I'll do it if I must
For me it's just another day of building faith and trust!

Patricia Baker
Lompoc, CA

June

In the cable of every wish;
Fear her one true friend;
Her mind wound tight with shame.

Judgment her one trusted strength;
No rest for the wicked;
She's lost to the ebb and flow of blame.

Her sons call to her in dismay;
Sins of the mother and the like;
The outer world has made its claim.

One day peace will come;
Truth will reign;
Love will shine away her pain.

Sharon L. Hall
Cincinnati, OH

Premonition

Dark November night
Envelopes me in a fog
My eyes cannot penetrate
But that watches
From every angle
The air is quiet
Nothing moves
The trees
Bare skeletons
Bony fingers reaching to the sky
Look down ominously
I step carefully
Knowing that silence
Is sometimes
The most dangerous sound
And clear my mind
Leaving it open
To instinct and intuition
Understanding
That there are things happening
And coming
Beyond physical perception

Michelle Zahner
Rockville, CT

The Curious Cow and the Furious Farmer

"What's wrong with the curious old cow?" Bill said
He looked and saw the curious cows head
Caught in the fence. Farmer Bill was furious
He wished his cow wasn't quite so curious.
The farmer took the cow by the horn
And led her back to the big red barn.
He placed the milking stool beside the cow
And started to milk her, when suddenly, "POW"
The curious cow just couldn't resist
A playful kick at a white kitty but missed.
The farmer jumped up and grabbed his big toe.
"That curious cow, has just got to go."
He loaded the cow in his big green truck
And took her to the Fair, "With luck,
I'll sell that cow for some money
Then, maybe I'll buy a fluffy little bunny."
His curious cow was missing from her stall
Farmer looked and listened for her bawl.
In the winners circle, he found his lost cow
With a blue ribbon hanging and taking a bow.
He took her home to his big red barn,
His curious cow with the curly horn.
Now, the farmer never gets furious
With his blue ribbon cow, no matter how curious.

Jane McManus
Yorktown, IN

Who Am I

Who am I
A simple question, yet I
Still pause and hesitate
Mull over and contemplate
Is there a label that
Easily defines me?
Who I've been and
Who I desperately want to be
Perhaps it is too early
To figure it out
As I go through this life
Filled with truths and doubts
But I know I'll have fun
Discovering who I am
I'm not done yet
Heck yeah, I've only just began

Bryana Flowers
Jackson, TN

Reverie

Not long ago,
The wind sang
In the early morning.

Dreams touched
You and I.
Half awake,
Your body curled
With mine.

Your breath flowed
Smoothly,
Gently.

Caressing your head,
I smiled
With memories
Of shared years.

My eyes faded,
Dreams again touched,
And your body
Curled with mine.

Gregory N. Mckulick
Pueblo West, CO

And Then

Fear
Teeming streaming tentacles squeeze the heart

Fear
Icy digits flood and fill, twist and probe the gut

Fear
Shivering, quivering mounds of jelly
Masquerade as hands and arms, legs and feet

And then

The wind shifts
The mood lifts

All is well again
And then
And then

Mary Mayer
Palm Coast, FL

Ask!

Now that God has found you,
Ask him to put his arms around you.
Ask that his divine peace surrounds you.
And, when troubles pile up and confound you,
Ask God's help…he will astound you!

Ivan D. Rinehart
Hot Springs, AR

Unborn Future

Her mother sleeps and dreams of a future.
Of the day she will see her baby's face for the first time.
The baby is deep inside her womb, for now,
But soon will be freed into the cruel world.
Her mother dreams of the day she will see her baby smile;
The day she will say her first "I hate you;"
The day she will wear a white dress and
Walk down the aisle, in love.
The baby girl is not yet born, but her future is.
A future made by God; with happy days,
Lots of laughing moments, and no regrets.
Still, her mother dreams a special future.
One filled with love, accomplishments, and colors.

Diana Yepishina
Pensacola, FL

Canadian Geese

We fly by night
We fly by day
Whether skies are blue or gray
Through rain or snow
We're on our way.

Our honking is heard by many
We let them know
We're flying high
Above the sky
People can see us flying by.

Sometimes we land on lakes and streams
We take a swim and sometimes eat
In fields of grass and aquatic plants
We have our fun and even rest
For another day passes, it's not the last.

William F. Koehler
Council Bluffs, IA

Pansies

Pansies:
Small, fancy,
Growing, dancing flowers,
Cool, beautiful, low, colorful
Dwarfs.

Sam Terray
Gainesville, GA

Survival

Oh, soul person of long ago,
You inspired me to reach deep into self
And rise above my nucleolus beginning
When faced with decisions, I always took
The easy way ~
You recognized how fragile I was,
And slowly nurtured me to comfort,
To being stronger and worthy,
Of the life we built together.
Now you are gone, whisked silently to heaven's door,
No more to influence greatness ~
Being gone, I whisper, "Nothing will ever be the same"
But with the great challenge you imparted in me,
Nothing changed ~ I am strong, and have lived a life of great reward.
I couldn't have done it without you.
You made me what I am today!

Sara R. Van Wormer
Elkhart, IN

Untitled

When you look into his eyes there is only one thing you can see:
Darkness.
That shows that he is gentle and loving.
Yet he is as strong as armor and as brave as a soldier.
He will carry me as long as he can,
So I shall love him as long as I can.
Whoever goes on first will receive tears from the other,
For we were closer than grass and dew.

Lydia B. Swinney
Lewisburg, KY

Untitled

Searching, my eyes dart around the room looking for signs of you.
The back of your head, silver and black hair reaching your shirt collar,
Trademark black sweater.
Are you here?
In and out of rooms I go, smiling,
Enjoying the company of others but wanting the possibility of you.
At the end of the day, you are there.
I approach you from behind, you turn and smile.
We talk.
You keep your distance as you step back from my directness.
Our eyes meet but once, you remember, I am sure.
A few words are spoken and then you walk away from us.
I am left standing alone, desperate to lose the memories.

Marsha H. Lupi
Ponte Vedra Beach, FL

Joey

If ever there was a boy
Who fills my heart with joy.

He's Joey with those big green eyes
If he was in a beauty contest,
He would win the prize.

When he hugs me and holds me so tight
I hug him back with all my might.

He likes to go to the park to play
He would love to stay out all day.

Everyone loves Joey, he's so cute
Even when he's running around in his birthday suit.

So here's to Joey with his great big smile.
We are going to walk that extra mile.

Grace Ervolino
Maspeth, NY

B. J. Quotes

It seems like now in my awkward mind
older days.
I can see and realize my mind destruction
ability in my youthful ways.

And now with God's enlightment, that I
have now been blessed.
I know the Journey for me is my faith
towards God being impressed

Bobby G. Johnson
Rutledge, GA

Year Two Thousand Eight

My age at eighty-three
Has a lot of memories
Many happy, some were not
Wedding vows proven
Can be hard to keep
Ours we kept for sixty-three
His last two days "2008"
Our family gave
Their love with care
We talked to him—did not
Know if he could hear
Eyes were not open to see
Left us all — "Memories"

Anna M. Craig
Fontana, CA

317

Thinking of Her

My chandelier, its spectrum invisible to the naked eye
has palpitations.
Let me go quickly then to the foothills of words
rising upwards, and not fling myself pointlessly
into that other territory beyond comprehension,
that place often mistaken for home
safe haven, sanctuary, place of adoration
that minefield
quicksand, precious trap.
Let me run now into a forest,
let me assume unknown animal grace
and light of foot leap with my old strength
into a thicket I can understand.
I'll build a fire and that will be my home.
I'll grow vegetables and eat wild fruit
and in spring when fall fish take my hook
I'll think of her and the taste
of wet paper bag salted,
damp cold fish eye staring ceilingward
calculating seconds as they tick away.

Earl W. Lehman
Jessup, PA

A Path in the Garden

Hold on gently to the delicate little hand of the carefree child within
yourself.
Let her be the one who guides you down your path of life.
Because if we aren't paying her attention we can, without realizing it,
let go, releasing her, and as she skips away occasionally
stopping to pick a single daisy she turns and calls your name
only to find you gone.
A fork in the road had lured you to go a separate way and since you can
no longer hear her sweet innocent voice calling you to follow,
sadly she saunters on down her path which led to the garden of
truth.
As she pulls petals from the dew kissed daisy she whispers to herself,
"She loves me, she loves me not. She loves me…she loves me not."
Petals flutter in the breeze like the delicate wings of a monarch,
eventually falling to the earth.
No more petals, no more wings.
Alone in the beautiful garden a small child cries, for she has lost her best
friend.
She dries her tears and prays to the Goddess.
Maybe one day she will find her way back.
So, advice for the young at heart.
Hold her little hand close to your heart.
In your mind where she goes, allow her laughter to fill your head, her
innocence to warm your soul, her magical being to embrace and
carry you with her into the garden.

Marion Wilson
St. Louis, MO

With Love From Mom

This long journey is not over it has just begun.
Do not think I have gone too far from you.
He has called me to begin my faithful work.
Pulling me, and so I shall follow.
Every sunny day, through the cloudy sky, I see you with my watchful
eye.
I see me in you with every smile in tiny shining eyes.
Lay me to rest my children for I will be waiting.
Crisp fluffy pillows are my loving arms.
Do not think I have gone too far from you.
Father time has called me from you.
Beating hearts, warm embraces, still remembering your tiny faces,
looking up at me from mom's embraces.
But, still do not think I have gone too far from you.
Tiny tummies, little toes, pulling me so I shall never really go.
Over here family's loving arms whom before we came, helping me
watch over you.
Through Sunbeams, flowers, rainbows in the sky.
I am idly waiting by.
Do not think I have gone too far from you.
So remember Mamma loves you…forever my pudding pies.

Khristina L. Ciaramella
Greenville, OH

Painful Goodbyes

Grey scruffy pigeons
Fall down from the sky
Echoing the poor girls tears
That pour from her eyes
And sweep everything far, far away

And even though time will make
The wound that doesn't show
Outside but in, fade
It will still be there to call up
Like a puckered scar it does not

Completely Disappear
But waits silently like
An assassin
Waiting to catch
Other's hearts only to break them

And leave them only
Slightly stitched up
Waiting for one lone breath
Or one
Memory
To open it up anew again.

Elana Young
Long Beach, CA

Childhood

Childhood is playing four square in the middle of the street until
darkness starts to settle in.
Childhood is cuts, scrapes, and bruises from rollerblading down the
biggest hill in the neighborhood.
Childhood is when Barbie and Polly Pocket is a girl's best friend.
Childhood is when Mommy and Daddy can fight away all your fears.
Childhood is when boys had cooties, and you would have to chant
circle, circle dot, dot now I got my cootie shot, square, square
now I got it everywhere.
Childhood is when you think your world is going to tumble down when
baby sister is coming.
Childhood is making forts with all the blankets in the house.
Childhood is Saturday morning cartoons, and a humongous bowl of
Cocoa Pebbles.
Childhood is playing bubble gum, bubble gum in a dish in the
schoolyard at recess.
Childhood is a pure innocence and bliss.

Jessica Strickler
Karthaus, PA

Forever Yours

Each and every anniversary with you
Is living my dream come true

As I remember the vows we said together
On that special day will always last forever

Good and rough times which has happened through the years
Both have brought us plenty of hugs and tears

But our continued love for each other
Has brought us closer together

So as we go forward like a team
Lets keep living our life long dream

Karen Norton
Findlay, OH

My Cowboy and I

My cowboy and I parted today
I didn't know the price I would have to pay
If only would I have been more true
I would not be unsettled here, alone and blue

Now I sadly bewail that cowgirl song
Pining and remembering all day long
Wondering whether he would return to me
I would keep the vow I said so solemnly

I little did know he already knew
That I was lonesome with little to do
He made the first move to come my way
Now I sing praise beside him each day

Arm in arm we walk through the day
Happily singing and dancing, blessing we pray
I thought when I met you, I could always be true
Love woke my heart to know, my cowboy was you.

Love like ours should never die
Uniting hearts as one to reach on high.

Joan Mays
West Brooklyn, IL

As a child Joan discovered there was an unexplored universe that needed storytelling.
She asked, "What else?" Her mother read aloud tales of people, animals, plants and
invention. Joan loves to write uplifting poems, essays and songs. "My Cowboy and
I" clarifies romantic images in peoples' minds. People love but often don't express
out loud. Listening to, saying or doing God's loving words can change worldly global
thought and reduce negative inclinations. Joan's interests are raising food plants, sharing
anniversaries, birthdays, participating in music bands, choirs. Raised in Lake Station,
Indiana, inspired by shoreline sand dunes.

The Ocean

The ocean
Is mother nature
The sea is the womb
I am a water baby
I embrace the quiet
White clouds floating by
Painted against the blueness of sky
I dive into the crystal clear
Bluegreen waters
I am as free and happy as I can be
Splashing around like a fish
Being at one with the sea
Back on the beach within reach
Laying on the soft sand
I hold an egg-shaped stone in my hand
In an instant, my entire life, I can understand
Light as a feather, away I can fly
Listening to the sound of seagulls cry
I've already been to heaven
I never have to die…

Christopher Tyrone
Yonkers, NY

Has the World Gone Mad?

Has the world gone mad?
I do believe it is so.
People abusing their power like it's the next fad,
Others turning their heads as if they don't know.

What's the world coming to?
Many soldiers are on the front lines,
While criminals advance with plenty to do;
And other not getting by in these times.

Where has all the money went?
The poor are scrounging for diapers and food,
While the big dogs can't account for money they've spent.
The world is turning gray with a gloomy kind of mood.

Are things really fair in love and war?
Our loved ones are dying because of this.
That can't be fair to the family's; that's sure,
As they grieve for the ones that they miss.

For the end of this truthful admission;
I give you my tears of joy and happiness,
Because one day the government will crumble into submission;
And end this game of depression and distress.

Amberly D. Napier
Columbus, IN

Friendship

Scream it out. Release the weight you must bear
You've been tricked into buying this hideous Nitemare
Understanding Come from a far away tilt
God should be the only one Judging our guilt.
I'll buy You a choir, I'll sing your name in Praise
I'd hire a hitman if I thought your Pain Could be erased.
I'd surrender to the devil so You could walk with your loved ones
Yup I'd suffer damnation to give you to your loved ones
If I knew the Cure for the disease Running through Your veins
I'd climb the mountains in Hades to inject it into your Fate
Whenever you feel down go ahead and take with.
Suffering and Joy go hand in hand with true friendship.
Give me a minute, I'll try stealing a miracle or two
I'd do anything Becky to keep my Friendship with you.

Veshelle T. Howell
Denver, CO

We Are Sisters

We are sisters, like JOY to the world.
That means forever sharing this gift given to us girls.
I see you smile deep inside those eyes so blue.
And pray to God our Father to keep watching over you.
Each wandering trip you take whenever you can "fly,"
Reminds me how much you enjoyed LIFE and it makes me want to cry.
So I gift you with my Angel—Peanuts by name.
So He can also guide you through this time of struggle and pain.

My heart goes out to you in a flash—the hottest ever known. (But this
one doesn't make me want to laugh.)
We shared 63 years and flashes of all sorts…
Happy hours with laughter, sighs that made us snort.

You are forever in my soul and I'm reaching for your hand,
Just one-more-moment would be really grand.

They say there is a BRIDGE…a way to reach your heart.
I pray for such a moment because you were with-me from my start.
You named Me after your favorite doll:
What more can I say?
We grew up 2-gether and made plans 2-grow-old that way.
But as God made other plans for us we have nothing ELSE to say.
God's Love to you for ever.
And may He always bless our ever-loving family with peace and
happiness.

Barbara J. Ravanelli
Milwaukee, WI

Alzheimer's Disease devastates every body and soul connected to each patient being robbed of their dignity. Today there are over 5 million people diagnosed in the USA. Please give a moment and a prayer. "We Are Sisters" is my coping-and-hoping (co-hoping) way to deal with watching her roam aimlessly up and down the little hallway she travels 24-7…unable to reach her. She keeps saying, "I want to go home." However, she is clueless as to what or where home really is. Trying to keep the FAITH, we keep praying that God grant her a quiet and happy hour in life and in death.

Max's Toys

Here's the big news! Here's the big scoop!
Joyce has a cat that plays with his poop!

He bats it around as it rolls on the floor
And it's there to greet Joyce as she comes in the door.

"Oh, Max," said she. "Have you found a new toy?
And while I've been gone, have you been a good boy?

Just what is this little brown ball that you've found?
It's not usually a thing I have lying around."

Then she picked it right up and squeezed it a bit
And cried out at the cat, "Oh my God! This is sh--!"

Now Joyce is still mad and thinks Max is a bum
But she picks up his "toys" before company comes.

This story is true, as for Joyce we still kid'er,
'cause she's got a cat who finds "toys" in his litter!

Bonnie Dick
Clyde, OH

The Song of the Doves

You never see them after dark
Where do they hide?
Perhaps they change their appearance
They're spiritual beings inside
They watch us day by day
Without us knowing
They help us with our decisions
Without their true identity showing
Lost in the morning mist they gather
I go out to feed the birds again
Mysteriously they appear around me
They are my very special friends
The master has a plan
That only He and nature know
If we listen very closely
We can hear the rhythm flow
Everything has a purpose
Every flower and bird a reason
Every year there are slight changes
To your life and nature's seasons
Listen very closely
To their cooing sound above
They call to tell us they are here
The song of the Dove

Theresa A. Thompson
Ft. Lauderdale, FL

From the Maker

When the thunder threw
down their spears and the
rain watered the earth with
tears, did he smile his work
to see? Did he who made the
sheep make me.

Jahdoran Hickling
Brooklyn, NY

Hills

I like hills—
They seem so contentedly ensconced
As they occupy their place in the landscape.
They accept the trees' bare branches in winter,
Letting those shadows enhance their contours.
They liven with spring's crowning of new green leaves,
Rest indulgently as autumn brings them flaming glory,
And wear winter's snow cover as a royal mantle,
Accepting, luxuriating with each successive season.
They remain serene, unyielding yet communicating
A sense of something I can't quite put into words.
Peace? Stability? A sense of eternity?
I only know I like hills—they lift my spirit.

Barbara E. Bogert
Asheville, NC

You Will Always Be Mine

When you walked into my life not too long ago;
I looked into your eyes and knew that I should never let you go.

When one finds their true love,
The heart will just know.

Oh, my darling, you will always be mine.
Your love has touched my heart and soul
more than you will ever know.
You will always be mine.

I could not even know that you would be the one.

All I could think to do was turn away and run.

It's so hard in life to find your true love;
But now I am sure you're an angel sent from up above.

We now have shared so many things in our life we've had together.

I'd do it all again, if I could be with you forever.
Even when our time ends, you will always be mine.

Melissa M. Heil
Benson, AZ

Southern Colloquials

I wear the hand-me-down countenance of my
Grandfather like an old pea coat in winter.
Eloquent voices of the south like:
I'm sick as a yellow dog.
Grits is South Carolina ice cream.
He is strong as a white mule
And up-to-par and
Katy bar
Embellish my stride.

My children will fit snug into these anthems.
They'll know that if you cut the head off a
Snapping turtle and nail it to a tree and
Touch a pair of pliers to its beak,
It will snap it out of your hand and won't let go
Till lightning strikes.

Let the thunder and lightning haunt the Southern
Sky, so I can use the pliers again to fix the
Closed-faced reel for tomorrow. I will go to the
Pond and hope a dragonfly lands on my rod to
Rest.

James Groome
Lenoir, NC

A New Dawn

They say we are entering a long recession
We are prone to anxiety and deep depression
We are feeling so much anxiety and doubt
But listen and I will tell you there's a way out
Hold to your faith and believe in eternity
And know that a better life is a certainty
This life we live is only a dream and a test
While we are on this earth we are only a guest
When we leave this place we'll wake up to a new life
A place where there is no hunger, sorrow or strife
You have to trust that you can make it through the fire
Even if things seem so hopeless and utterly dire
Those whose love and belief in God is strong and pure
These are the elect who will make it and endure
He will hold their hand and walk with them through the fire
They will keep going through it all and will not tire
We grieve for our children and their future sorrows
We worry for them and for their tomorrows
We have to hold them, love them, and teach them to pray
Give them to God and trust He will show them the way
Peace and security seem so out of our touch
We desperately long for it, we need it so much
Stay strong, keep the faith and always keep going on
And hold to the promise of a brighter new dawn

Linda Miller
Johnstown, OH

334

John's Travel Wish

It was raining that night
Dark clouds all around
The conductor calling out
The train was "everywhere" bound
Ever since John was a child
He wanted to see the world
Flying the air ways
Even diving for pearls
In a small town
John didn't see very much
But to see all of God's creations
John's heart is touched
John worked hard every day
And without a doubt
Began realizing the dream of
Traveling east, west, north, and south
His chance finally came
With luggage packed and ticket in hand
The destinations once dreamed of
Were all going as planned
But god had other plans
That john didn't know of
God gave him the best
Travel destion, heaven above

Venus S. Luna
Martinez, CA

Poem for Humanity

If everyone looked inside their soul
I think that they would find
A way to impact others
Just by being kind.

It doesn't require a grand gesture
Or spending more than you can afford
Sometimes all people really need
Is a smile or an understanding word.

For many, life is a constant struggle
Due to reasons beyond their control.
They persevere and endure the hardship
Searching for hope that has yet to unfold.

For others, life is a blissful walk
Down a path lined with blessings and grace.
They breeze through life and never know
The challenges that others must face.

It seems there ought to be a way
To achieve balance among all mankind.
If people realized the power of compassion,
The selfishness epidemic would decline.

Laurie Teague
Elkton, MD

Continued Growth

I am oppressed with conflict in my heart!
I am naked in lust!
Yet, I remain objective in this process . . .

C.O.N.F.L.I.C.T.

As I pave my path, I gather chucks of faith and kisses of inspiration.
I embrace this transformation . . . my "yin to my yang."

The conflict of lust and love stomping my body as if it were a herd of
wild mustangs, approaching quickly!

Deeply.
I soak my desire with the blankets of nakedness.

A renewed power lies softly beside me.

So I am faced with this light side of my dark lust.

Love continues to grow.

De'Anna Quillen
Fullerton, CA

40 Weeks

No-show, oh no! The test, then yes.
Tell him, so grin. Thirty-five, oh God, why?
Prenatal, am I able? Weight gain, mood swings?
Can someone push me from the table?

Step on the scale, pee in the cup.
Hey, Doc, how many more months
Will I be throwing up?
More tests, blood, glucose, ultrasound, wow!

I know I'm too old for this now!
I used to fit this dress, what's happened to my breasts?
The final days have come; I can't wait to wear my thong!
This is a special time, you see, God put a life in me.
So, I must wait and wonder what he or she will be.

Labor pains, water break, more pains,
Breathe, Mother, breathe.
Three, six, nine, ten, head, shoulder, twist, then feet.
What?! Push again for the "placenta?" Lord, God, why me?
It's a cry, then a sigh. Is it a boy or a girl?

Only forty weeks will tell . . .

Cynthia Harrison
Steger, IL

338

Beyond Closed Smiles

Peering into their faces, smiles abeam
Posing there, giving a come hither bid;
Asking for acceptance by all, I gleam
In perfect petrified reflection kid.
Inside, looking out, outside coming in
Giddy, as if mesmerized by twinkle lights;
Before me is a party filled with kin.
I brought mine, they bring theirs in joyful plight;
Is this a death to wondering "what if?"
Stepping into the swirling swarm we core,
Touching, gifting, loring in gentle riff;
Placing separated souls upon the floor
Our cheeks soften, the lips relax, teeth show;
Beyond closed smiles, tender tended senses flow.

Nancy R. Miller
Claremont, CA

As an adopted person I was miraculously reunited with my birth family after a fifty-five year separation. It was my birth-sister Betsy who connected the locked-away dots of my unconscious past. During our three months together we uncovered our shattered family history, reconnected with our birth mother and three brothers and we created a sisters bond, a safety net as Betsy and I faced her sudden illness and impending death. This poem expresses the insights gained during visits with my birth family. It appears in my 258-page Novel Memoir presently undergoing rewrites and edits.

Heart of Steel

Through my window,
I watch the seasons pass me by,
I've had my battles in life,
But God has silenced my cries.

My courage burns like fire
In the dark and lonely night,
Melting away the wounds of yesterday,
Pain I no longer have to fight.

'Cause I'm a warrior inside
With a heart of steel,
I fight with passion
To turn my dreams into something real.

My fears have been captured
By the strength I behold,
I've defeated the depression
That once rested deep in my soul.

And the angels have saved me,
Bringing me mercy in the end,
I've survived the war of misery,
I've awoken from the dead.

'Cause I'm a warrior inside
With a heart of steel,
I fight with passion
To turn my dreams into something real.

Sarah Haass
Central Islip, NY

Not in My Dictionary

Don't even try to find Selfish,
Ungrateful will never be seen here;
There is space neither for Arrogance or Prejudice,
Nor hatred, malice, or dread.
I have no definition of Jealousy;
Foolish appears not in my source.
Greed and Distrust lack pronunciation,
Having no spelling or syllables at all.
Discrimination also could be part of my thinking,
Affecting what I hear, say, and see,
However, just like the other aforementioned words
It is not in my dictionary.

Jonathan Scott
Bronx, NY

To God be the glory for blessing me with the skill to express myself through poetry. I am much more articulate on paper than I am speaking, as are most of the Scott family. The main theme of this poem is to tell the reader who Jonathan really is, according to the perceptions of loved ones, friends, and co-workers. By telling others who I'm not (not in my dictionary), I'm actually revealing who I truly am if you get to know me well enough.

Chance

The world is mine to wander in
And dreams are mine to choose.
But life is just a game of chance
And I may win or lose.
For I may play the hand I hold
Or toss the cards away.
And still there is no certainty
The sun will shine today.
I may be bold or hesitant
And either path I take
May be the more successful one
For my peculiar sake.
Yet somewhere as I go along
I surely must decide
And well I know I ought to let
My conscience be my guide.
But whether I am satisfied
To linger or advance
The wheel of fortune goes around
And I must take a chance.

Barbara Schimidt
Yucaipa, CA

Deep into the Forest

Deep into the forest, a sacred land
Untouched by the claws of Man
Hidden behind a veil of trees
Protecting a throne like kings and queens

There is much to discover and many mysteries uncovered
The rain
It magically appears then fades
Like liquid crystal falling
From a blanket of feathery clouds falling
Exotic creatures with curious eyes
Play underneath a moonlit sky
They frolic through gardens paved in gold
Everything is alive and breathing
Quenching the thirst of a restless soul
At night, you can hear a pulse beating

Deep into the forest spirits sing
A collision of rhythm and harmony
Songs of love and loss
Songs that civilization forgot
Singing songs of survival

Danette Stowers
Lawndale, CA

When Will I Know?

Who am I is still the question that I want
Answered, but it is not a simply answered question,
But an evolving enigma
Containing a beginning but no end,
Nor a definition, rhyme or reason.
So who is this person?
Is it a moon, a lion or human?
Is she loyal, clever, talented or
None of these? Am I ruthless, charming, spoiled,
Loving, ugly, outgoing, selfish, or
Maybe I'm not adventurous, perfect, creative, wicked,
dependent, nor sure.
When in my lifetime will I ever know?
One day an answer will reveal and show.

Gitla Shooster
Beverly Hills, CA

In Storage

The first year, the birds
lited on my toys of childhood:
picture books, baby dolls, and refrigerator art,
in storage.

The second year, the squirrels
ran across my decorations
of my teen years:
posters, stylish clothes, assigned novels, and fashion dolls,
in storage.

The third year, the snakes
slithered over my goals
of early adulthood:
photographs, lecture notes, boy toys, and vehicles,
in storage.

The fourth year, the mice
scampered over the materialism of middle age:
graduate schools, careers, relationships, and politics,
in storage.

The fifth year, the birds,
squirrels, snakes, and mice
returned to convene over my corpse,
in storage.

Billie G. Malsbury
Brookhaven, MS

Loved Colors

roses are red so very true
just like my love for you

water is blue full of chills
like what I get when I see you by the sunset on the hills

flames are orange gracefully moving
just like when we're together it's very soothing

stars are bright white, silver, and gold hovering the sky
just like us dancing all night

so our love is true
I will seal it gratefully with a kiss upon you

Hannah Brandanger
Breezy point, MN

Hope Throughout History

Hope will motivate men
Silently compelling time again
Mankind seeks a better life
Free from persistent strife

Dreaming is nothing new
Ancient man did it too
He crossed glaciers on foot
Hunting game in pursuit

Let my people go
Mass exodus from Egypt's pharaoh
Eventually lost for forty years
New lands transcend tears

Our forefathers sought
Liberty purchased through blood lost
Casting independence bell to ring
Separation from the king

Shackled men were bought
Divided national war was fought
Deep wounds made healing long
Admitting we were wrong

Candidates for the highest office
Visions of what is best
Uncertainty beyond view or scope
Man's motivation is hope

Bruce E. Marshall
Bluffton, OH

347

Nature's Gleam

Birds in flight
Welcome the dawn,
As the sun shines
On a new delight,
Soft winds blow,
Greeting the flowers
That blossom in the light.

On a bright summer's day,
Children play
In open fields and vast plains.
Beyond green pastures, past rolling hills,
Lovers dance to music echoing in the valley,
Harmony and rapture abounding.

Sailing through the ocean blue,
Along miles of calm, rippling seas,
The atmosphere is serene.
A red-orange glow sparks over the horizon,
As the sun sets on the ocean floor,
A warm feeling surrounds me on this distant shore.

Simple pleasures from Nature's treasures,
Never cease to amaze me,
Dazzle in the glow,
And behold,
Pleasant scenes in Nature's gleam.

John G. Falber
Keansburg, NJ

I was born in Manhattan, New York. I remember as a child, enjoying the view of nature while walking in the park with my father on Saturday afternoons. As an avid lover of nature, I wrote this poem to express my awe of our beautiful world, where the simplest of wonders can make us feel astonishment. I am grateful and I thank God for such beauty shown to me.

You Make Me Happy

The one thing I'd do
is anything for you.
When you touch me the way you do,
I love you more and more like I intended to.
I didn't know love actually existed,
until the day that I met you.
I am just so attached like glue.
You mean everything to me,
I just wish you could see
How happy you make me.
You make me happy,
even when the mood is calm.
You make me happy because,
this is where I belong.
You bring out a totally different side of me,
and I love it, I really do.
Just not as much as I have come to love you.
I love you so much,
I just hope you know
that I am invariably thinking of you,
as my life tends to grow.
You are what I call mine,
and therefore, I am yours.
You take away my pain,
because of my heart, which you contain.

Amber N. Fine
New Eagle, PA

Mother's Song

The shadows whisper
And lightning dances
With each gray drop
She has increased your chances

Bolting here and crashing there
The lightning dances in the air

As is a beacon to signal the spring
Flowers awake and birds to sing
Mother Nature reigns with her natural beauty
Caring for her children with a loving swoon

Out goes winter
In comes spring
And summer soon

Chris Allen
Columbia, TN

If I Could Follow the Sun

Tonight I stood upon my balcony
Just watching the beauty of the sun
I watched it as it slowly went down
As another day is done

In the daytime I feel the warmth of the sun
But when the day is through
I know I have to say goodbye
And give my sun back to you

In the night when I sleep upon my pillow
My dreams see you dancing in the sun
I see the sun reflect off of you
And I know that you are the one

I wish there was a way to go with the sun
Because then I would be with you
But if I cannot make that journey
Your morning sun will have to do.

Crystal Garcia
Elkhart, IN

December Eve

Star light, star bright
On this cold December eve night
As I'm about to see
Our first snowflakes indeed

Star light, star bright
Snowflakes falling in the night
Twinkling as they fall
All dressed up in their awe

Star light, star bright
Snowflakes dancing in the night
Swirling and whirling—Oh! What a sight
To my eyes this was just right

Star light, star bright
Where did the snowflakes go?
In all their radiance so
As well as their abundant glow

Star light, star bright
I guess you're gone for now
In this snowy little town
Of all white on the ground

Star light, star bright
Oh! What a nice sight
To see you again in flight
On a cold December eve night

Betsy Mulligan
Clinton, MD

Flag Day

With patriotic pride our country gleams victorious,
The American flag waves high, spectacular, and glorious!
Red, white, and blue hues ripple gently and free.
God bless America, how we love thee!
Let's salute this special emblem
In a manner that will show
Liberty, truth, and justice,
And forever it will flow!

Judy Golin
Brooklyn, NY

Brooklyn, New York is a good place to live. I was born and raised here, blessed with 68 years of life. I like to dance, love to sing, but most of all I enjoy writing poetry. I have two great sons and a wonderful daughter-in-law. My five grandchildren, Jon, Gody, Erica, Andrew, and Henry are the apple of my eye. God bless you all and God bless America.

Tribute to Life

At this wonderful age of seventy-one
My life is not over, it's barely begun.
Now I have time to reminisce
Of all the joys I didn't miss.
A newborn child, such an innocent joy
Whether a delicate girl or a sturdy boy.
When I awake each morning and see the skies
I marvel at the beauty I see with these eyes.
How green the grass, how bright the sun!
Yes, I know for sure life has just begun.
Yet if it's cloudy and I hear the rains,
The sound is soothing as it strikes the panes.
The seasons change as everyone knows,
Soft snow floats down as north winds blow.
The beauty it scatters as it hits the ground
Dresses the world in white without a sound.
Then I think back in times gone past,
All was not easy…but good memories last.
Isn't that what's important in the lives we live?
We reap all the joys if we are willing to give.
As I see life at seventy-one
I'm thankful I feel that now it's begun.
We all know that we can't stay here forever,
But, be sorry we lived? No never, no never!

Shirley A. Zimmerman
Lebanon, PA

Prisoner

We are all prisoners of some kind,
Even if it is just of the mind.
Driven by opinions, thoughts, and attitudes,
Of which sometimes not so prudent.

Victims of affairs of the heart,
To the wind we throw caution.
Ruled by a passionate fire,
Too often the outcome is dire.

Slaves to the March of Time,
To the body be so unkind.
Day in day out—year in, year out,
It pays no heed to our circumstance.

Shackled by past mistakes,
Unable or unwilling to make the break.
Regret from chances missed
Persistent wonder—"What if?"

Some dreams realized,
Many dreams lost.
Either way your pay the piper,
Stark reality the cost.

Prisoners in our velvet cells,
Echoes in a wishing well
Free will and choices made,
Make us prisoners of ourselves and fate.

Sammye J. McLane
Lubbuck, TX

My Destiny

Ah! Tis my destiny to suffer much.
What did I do Lord to deserve your frenzied touch?
You shaped me, and molded me, and gave me life.
I've put up with much toil and strife.

I've tried to do the best I can.
But a wall protruded every which way I ran.
When I tried to be happy I became morose.
Is something missing, do you suppose?

And then I felt your presence Lord.
"I've been with you always" He said, "since you were born.
I molded you perfectly, don't you see?
What took you so long to come to me?"

"Now that you know me your troubles will be less,
You can lean on me and you will be blessed.
If I'd made life easy, you'd still be lost.
But now you know me, your no longer tossed."

I asked for forgiveness for my every wrong.
For doubting His presence for so very long.
My heart filled with joy and a love so great!
I'm expecting miracles, my destiny, my fate.

Florence Schwingle
Menomonie, WI

I am just a housewife and mother of six. I am now eighty-five years old and I'm just
getting started with my career. One day when I was alone and didn't know what to do,
I started writing. Soon, I had written a poem that surprised even me. I enjoyed it so
much that I wrote another poem. Pretty soon I had written a book full of poetry. My
friends asked me how I could do this, and this was my answer: I didn't write it alone
God inspired me to do it and it's one of His blessings. Growing old isn't so bad when
you have a hobby.

356

Hold This Tongue

Dear Lord, please keep my tongue in line.
Hold the lead
To the reckless steed
That is this tongue of mine.

Give my tongue a bridle, Lord.
Govern its every move
Until all my tongue's words, the complete horde,
Is nothing of which You would disapprove.

'Tis this mouth that's shoving my emotions asunder,
Causing me to slam into many a spiritual blunder.
This tongue has almost drowned my relations with my sister,
Almost suffocated my sisterhood. This is as obvious as sounding thunder.

If my words are as snowy messengers' steeds,
Racing from my lips to see to folks' needs…
I'll let them pass, but
If my words are as brunette battle steeds, please remind me to lock my
"oral gates" shut.

Lord, I know that it's my responsibility
To keep this tongue that You so graciously gave me
Under my feeble scrutiny. In this area, please help me.
Thanks for listening to this prayer from me.

Hannah R. Minks
Brinson, GA

I am a seventeen year old girl with Cerebral Palsy. I live with my two siblings and our parents. I'm in tenth grade in a college prep program. I write poetry as a hobby. I wrote "Hold this Tongue" after a fight I had with my sister. I was feeling guilty for yelling during the fight and since I am a Christian bought with a price, I wrote my poem as a prayer to God for help holding my tongue.

357

About Inspiration

I bottled inspiration through the years
Just as I bottled coins and fireflies and marbles as a kid
All tears and joys and colors that rise within the heart
I captured, and did as part of what we all do:
I opened the lid later on and counted what I had.
Rainbows and sunsets came tumbling out; the woman next door
My mom, dad, pets, friends. The lore
Of all I'd read—memories—the balm of all I'd lived
In a mixture with what I felt and who I am today.
But like Pandora's box opened, spilling evil throughout the land,
My inspiration couldn't be recaptured.
Like a higher hand had made it part of me.
Thought alone can bring it back and any lack I feel
Within a time can be a ray of sunshine if I but apply
My escaped bottle-stuff. All good can be mine in those rough times
If I see the rainbows shining through and in lieu of them
Which bear bad moment, I sprinkle them with stardust, and I find
A kinder, gentler place to live within my mind.

Natalie Jo Barnett
Sierra Vista, AZ

Sailboats

Sailboats are all afloat
From east to west
The lines of which we test
For the breeze is true
And the water, the sea, it is so blue
Harmoniously rising with each wave, we go
up and down, from which we flow
Sailboats are like life you see
The lives of time between he and thee
Blessed assurance Jesus is mine
But for a life so dear, for a life so fine
The sailboats on which we can go
Sailing away on the seas a flow
I love the Lord I know
So sail on, on the seas of change
Braving waves, like when life itself becomes rearranged
Sailing, its time is true
Like the color of the ocean, the color that is still blue
Freedom tells us that there still is time
Time to "sail on" and still time to shine
Praying always for strength in the Lord for the chance
The chance to still "sail on," the chance to dance
On sailboats.

Cathy J. Drummond
Hallandale Beach, FL

Naked Cowboy—A New York Icon

Standing in Downtown Manhattan, all summer and all winter long
There is a man called Naked Cowboy, who sings his endless cowboy
songs
All day long, he's standing there, in cowboy boots and underwear
He doesn't need to stay in style, wearing little but a smile

Strumming the strings, strumming the strings
One of New York's oddest things

As the city's crowds look on and gaze, this man will never cease to amaze
Thousands of people stop and stare, to see Naked Cowboy on his derriere
Listening to this cowboy croon, it's clear his voice is out of tune
He and his guitar will sing out loud, drop me some coins I sure ain't proud

Strumming the strings, strumming the strings
One of New York's oddest things

A testament to modern culture, like a nearly naked singing sculpture
Get your picture with this strange Adonis, whose offbeat style's thrust
upon us
When first seeing him from afar, you hope he doesn't move his guitar
His voice rises above the city's din, accompanied by too much skin

Strumming the strings, strumming the strings
One of New York's oddest things

His BVDs make him unique, with little else covering his physique
His oddly chosen path to wealth, could cause many problems to his health
I must admit he is most entertaining, but wish his clothes were more
restraining
If in New York go to Times Square, at a grand a day, he'll sure be there

Strumming the strings, strumming the strings
One of New York's oddest things

Chris Besser
Pittsburgh, PA

Old Men

Old men, grim men
Silent men, unsmiling men
Sitting together, huddled
Three on a bench
What thoughts have these?
Any happy memories that
Might bring some joy or
Only grim reminders of
Past loss and unhealed wounds
Unwilling to chance some
Pleasure as time quickly
Goes by

Doris H. Chaffee
Tucson, AZ

Spring

Hush my aching heart less my love you impart,
For she is Spring and belongs to May,
I'm December old and gray.
She is Spring its buds bursting forth,
Gay and frivolous heart beating wild,
Beauty and youth hers for a while.
I could love her until the end of time,
But she is Spring free as the wind,
And I am December this to remember,
No more to recapture the Spring of my rapture.

Grace M. Wheeler
Fontana, CA

Life

Life passes fast

Life comes slow

But life is on time

All the time

Even if it never happened

Leesa Peterson
Smithtown, NY

Winter Wonderland

Winter is here, the snow's on the ground
The crunch of each footstep brings
A cold frosty sound
The snowballs & snowflakes
Are fun for awhile
They bring childhood memories
Back with a smile
We're hoping this year will
Bring memories to you
And find peace in your heart
With your love anew

Linda Earl
St. Marys, OH

362

Please Don't Bring Me Back

Please don't bring me back,
to that scary, frightening town.
Where I flew the Blackhawk over,
and later was shot down.
My crew was all injured, except for one who's dead.
I hear so much gunfire, there is ringing inside my head.
Iraq is a place that no soldier wants to go,
where there's rubble in the streets and dust that will blow.
War is violent and to us we don't need,
for our soldiers to get shot,
then fall down and bleed.
I want to stay here at home with my family, kids, and wife,
where I can live in peace for the rest of my life.
There's one thing I ask of you Col . . .
it's about Iraq.
I did not like it one bit,
so please don't bring me back.

Joshua Hayes
Mason, OH

I'm in the tenth grade and I've been writing poetry ever since I can remember. I love to play sports and hang out with friends. A hobby of mine is drawing and poetry. I express myself through art. Poetry is in my blood. I have a younger brother and a younger stepbrother. My mom and stepdad work together. My real dad passed away when I was 14. What inspired my poem was my cousin Brandon who fought in Iraq. A few of his friends were killed in combat. I wrote this poem because I care about him a lot.

What Is My Purpose?

My purpose here, in mortality,
Is to prepare me, for immortality;
To be the best that I know how;
To do, what needs to be done, now;

To strive to leave a legacy;
To seek what I was born to be;
Then to listen to that inner voice;
That will help me make a choice,

That will prepare and initiate me
In all I need to do and be;
In order to those things create
In their imaginary state;

And after that, in reality
To become what I came here to be;
To fulfill my mission, here on earth;
To prove myself, to gain self worth;

To learn all that I need to know;
That in knowledge I might grow;
To God's principles review;
To put faith in Him, to seek what's true;

To trust in God and not in man;
To walk according to His plan,
Along the path, that eventually,
Will lead me where I hope to be—eternally!

Sara E. Thomas Gifford
St. George, UT

The Slippery Slope

Hello there. I can picture you now; staring down at that place, that bottomless slippery slope that leaves you longing for the sight of where it goes. You're tempted to walk down it but are ambivalent because of the anxiety and fear of where it leads.

But here I am down here, down in that black abyss looking up; trying to find a ray of light, struggling to keep my emotions of anger and frustration from pushing me further and further into that hole.

Where there is color and expression in your life, I experience nothing. I am caught in a labyrinth of depression and mood swings.
You want to help me, or at least a part of you does, but I can't see you and you can't see me. I have fallen too far down that slippery slope.

I am a boy in a well, or a prisoner without a future, hope or success. I grit my fingernails into the walls as they crumble down upon my recent progress. I am nothing to you and the others.

If I was something, I would be as insignificant as a clot of lint at the bottom of a laundry shoot. I cannot be helped without a vision.
I cannot be helped without a path. I will just be down here. Down here trying to climb this slippery slope, taking one step forward and two steps back.

Finally seeing a patch of light, and then watching it close back up leaving me blind and hopeless. Finally climbing to the near top ridge of the hole and tumbling down again leaving me deaf and doubtful. I am the mangled bird on the side of the street that everybody overlooks.

Devon DiPaolo
Boxborough, MA

Before Thanksgiving

I.

As two roads merge,
an open farm truck laden with crates
forge its way ahead of me.
Between the slats, red-combed heads
free themselves,
peering through to the world,
peering,
asking . . .

II.

On the Bahnhoffe to Treblinka,
As the train emerges
from the tunnel,
Hungry faces peer from boxed cars
peering,
asking . . .
Oh, dear ones, do not ask.

Adele Kamp
Croton on Hudson, NY

The Light

Light for the journey
Peace for the soul
God's love and mercy makes us whole.

It's His grace through faith
When the way seems hard
And the journey long
It's God's love that makes us strong.

It's the light for everyone
That shines in the darkness of this world.
That comes down from above
To give peace and love.

Elaine Ricks
Syracuse, NY

Mother gave us love as a child and the love for family life. Being inspired by the love of God and the study of the Bible, through trials and tribulations, the words flow from the heart giving thanks to God and praise.

Just as a Spirit

I watch you now
Just as a spirit
But I'm confused
You're crying so much
Why? Because of me?
Because I died?
But you said
You wouldn't care
If I left you today
Or even tomorrow
Yet you weep so much
What you think?
That I still be here?
No, you were wrong
You didn't care
No one did
Yet everyone cries
Because I didn't go on
With all the pain in my heart
I just needed one more reason
And you gave it to me
That's why I did this
But still you weep
With tears falling
Onto my frozen body
As I watch you
Just as a spirit

Christina Dunnington
Manassas, VA

Angels

They say that angels appear in so many places
And that they wear so many different faces
I never believed in angels until I met you
And then in my darkest hour I realized
They do exist. You were there it is true.
Your smile, your hug, your gentle touch,
I never knew they could mean so much
You are here now and here you will stay
to help me, to guide me until my final day.
And beyond that I ask only, PLEASE STAY.

Robert J. Leone
Waymart, PA

My writings concern two periods in my life. One the most terrible and one the most beautiful. Eleven years ago I lost my wife to cancer. I was devastated and felt there no longer was a reason for me to go on. Thoughts of taking my own life filled my mind. A close friend and co-worker saw my despair. She showed me understanding and compassion that I did not think was possible from another person at that time. Life began to have meaning again. On September 13, 2003, I married that special person and she is my special angel.

Death in Progress

...6th floor...ICU...I sit in the hallway just
outside of your room...waiting, endless waiting...
A nurse closes the curtain, what's happening?
Why did she do that? What's GOING ON HERE?
Are you there God? I trusted you, I gave it all
over to you, God! I put it in your hands...
He's only 22, it's NOT supposed to be like this!
Not MY son...This isn't SUPPOSED TO BE
HAPPENING! I tell myself you'll be ok...
I mean... you HAVE to be ok, right? RIGHT?
...7:25am...I am frozen in time... what
day is it? It's February, but WHAT DAY IS IT?
I call your father working in North Carolina.
Somehow I hear the words I manage to choke out
"Come home, NOW, our boy is GONE," I sob...
I have to call your grandmother
I think I'm going crazy
I feel chaos in my brain
How will I tell your brother?
Why, God? He was so kind and gentle, why?
We love him and need him with us
I wish I could wake up... why can't I wake up?
I just want my son, please can I just have my son?
PLEASE!

Sherri Welch
Camillus, NY

What Made Him Great

He made her laugh
He believed
He bull-horned at the Twin Towers
He called for war

He ignored the vicious media
He laughed at the idiot comics
He smiled at the cunning politicians
He was the great "decider"

He made the hard decisions
He told the world the truth
He took a heroic stand
He acted to save a country

He stood up to terrorists
He saved the Middle East
He was the last great
Commander-in-chief

Shirley Moulton
Rockville, MD

Invisible

The world does not want to hear us,
So it turns its ear.
No one wants to hear our cries.
All we can do is try to run, run far away
Until our weary legs collapse
Or they catch us.
Don't you hear our cries?
Won't you look with your eyes?
Please help before they catch us.

Suzanne Rush
Greeley, CO

My Ancestors

My Irish ancestors had no sense of time.
They never hurried.
They saw no reason at all to hurry.
Why should anything be done quickly?
Why should something have to be finished
by a certain hour or date?
Why should anything ever be finished?
My Irish ancestors believed in eternity
which has no end and no beginning.
Eternity is the "is" state
where only the Irish know how to be.
God surely is Irish.
He just is.

Nora T. Donegan
Bronx, NY

Christmastime

Family and friends are coming.
I'm running from Uncle Davie
and his big sloppy kisses.
I need to be alone maybe.

The party has just begun.
Cousin Minnie and Mickey are fighting.
The snow has just fallen.
And I am running.

Chicken is being served.
Everyone is sitting and waiting.
This is our annual tradition.
And I am still running.

Christmas is supposed to be the most
wonderful time of the year.
But why am I like this?
Mom and Dad and baby Jenny are jolly.
During Christmas, I am not supposed to be like this.

Anjette Rostock
New York, NY

The Prisoner's Neognomation

A man addressing life in locks and crumpled forms upon the rocks,
Appraising glances cast from hawkish eyes to fools upon the stocks.
Staring deep in haunting hollow eyes that glare in colors sallow,
To glean of past and present locks the fate of waves upon the docks.
For the smoldering, sputtering chars of the haze,
And the scaffold age burn in the depths of His gaze.

A king and daughter child will go to ancient hill of craven crow,
To find the soothing sooth on snowy mountain faces, stones that know,
Every word in every telling, every tone in every singing,
Of villages set in snow and shone upon by angel's glow,
As the world in apocalyptical craze,
Will forget the revolving and twisting of the maze.

The icy bells of Pluto ring while tortured souls below must sing,
And serenade the earthly things as Elysian sings.
Praying peace upon the mountain, peace among the trees and fountains,
The bellows feed the flames of Olympian forges, smelting gold.
For the ornaments glided for Gods and the praise
Of the mortals and minstrels below in the haze.

Zachary Bourbeau
Tupper Lake, NY

Morning at the Ocean

The brisk air tastes salty,
and the water is cool.
Sand is stuck in my toes,
and there are miles of tide pools.

The horizon is set aflame,
as the sun aims for the sky.
People are already swimming,
and sun tan lotion some apply.

Surfers have been lined up,
the games are about to begin.
They race through the dark waves,
and the tall blonde guy wins.

The seagulls are squawking,
as the silvery fish they greet.
My legs start feeling heavy,
so on the beach I take a seat.

you do not need to go shopping,
or any of that city commotion.
It is calm and surreal,
It is a morning at the ocean.

Victoria Howell
Springfield, VA

Where There Is a Will There Is a Way!

My neighbor Bill, a busy, diligent man,
cleared the plot of brush, and pulled the weeds,
The weeds he put in a large trash can,
this plot of land he turned into a veggie garden, even
saving some of it for the flowers:
The kind of vegetables numbered seven,
There were lettuce, radishes carrots, peas,
spinach, beans, tomatoes- lots of these
Bill is a man of neatness and order:
He erected a fence around the garden's border.
The watered, fertilized, tended garden grew, lush and green.
Bill's family helped, too.
Indeed, the tomatoes grew to the best I've ever seen!
No far from the garden lived a little long-eared hippity-hop;
He eyed the garden with yearning eyes,
Considering it to be his coming free grocery shop.
One day he came to this garden (this little, long-eared honey bunch).
But, the fence was high, the fence was tall, and he was so small.
Busily he dug under the fence with busy paws, went in—and had lunch.

Poet Ergol
Middle Island, NY

During these grim times, poetry—a form of music—softens and enhances our harsh lives.
Therefore, looking on events and occurrences with a poetic smile grows in importance,
especially using everyday words, avoiding convoluted highbrow language. As music,
poetry may have rhythm, rhyme, alliteration; it may take forms of quatrain, sonnet, etc.
But I hope to bring smiles, color, and laughter.

Snowflakes

Snowflakes falling
To the ground
See them swirling
All around—
The wind is howling
And blowing hard
Moving the snowflakes
All around—
Each snowflake that falls
Is of a different size
Some are small
And some are large
And some will even melt
Before they hit the ground—
As winter's cold air
Brings the snowflakes this year
You'll watch in Amazement
As they pile up on the ground.

J.D. Hanscome
Culpeper, VA

A Wish

In another world,
a few years ago,
things were so different,
I wish it weren't so.

Folks traveled freely,
not a thought of harm.
Trips were a pleasure,
no cause for alarm.

Plan your agenda,
pack clothes in your case.
Thoughts of a fine trip,
a smile on your face.

The fun to be had,
your own folks to see,
all the memories,
and what came to be.

May the time come soon,
when peace is at hand,
and we go safely,
through all of the land.

Victoria B. Dobson
Manchester, MO

Angel

O Angel closing over me
what do you think you truly see,
dreams or visions in future's past
on eternity's horizon where the die is cast?

Can you tell me of bliss, of some soulful love
in a nothing that's centered so far and above
or will I know but a moment of unreachable heaven
in each life that I live with a promise just given?

Will my ever be ended, or is it yet just my fate
once again to be searching, yet again touch the gate
and continue those journeys once then as before,
fulfill the renewal of the me just once more?

O Angel whisper my story, help me to see
more than visions or dreams, what I am and must be.
Guard the soul to that which I know to be true.
Guide me gently to each life that I'm destined to do.

Colleen Haddock
Firestone, CO

The Twin Towers

It must have been sad
That day in New York City
It was a day of sorrow
And a day of pity
Oh they must have cried
For the loved ones that had died
Because when the people screamed
And the wind howled
There was someone weeping in the crowd
When the daylight faded and the people settled down
An awful smell came from the crowd
A smell of blood, a smell of tears
A smell that would even hurt your ears
The smell of smoke
The smell of dust
It was the smell of sorrow
That came upon us
Around the country people wept
Trees would moan
As they slept
The birds did not tweet instead
They just hung their head
For it had been a sad day
In the USA.

Evan Biedermann
Baldwinsville, NY

If Only, Is for People Who Live in the Past

If only, I said what I meant
If only, what was the intent
If only, is for people who live in the past.
Me, I am a future person. I know I cannot move
forward looking behind. What is behind can never
be relived, therefore why waste the time.
Life is to be lived to the fullest without
regret for what might have been. Sure life
will have many stop lights, speed bumps and
road blocks; just drive slowly across the barriers
and keep your eyes on the straight and narrow road.
If there is a stop sign at the corner, look both ways
and please take the road that lead to the destination
your heart had always dreamed of. But if, for some
unforeseen reason, the road you have chosen is the
wrong one, fear not: at least you can say, I TRIED.
As you sit in your rocker in the sunset years of your
life, your heart is content and you do not have to say
IF ONLY:

Gwendolyn Wilson
Laurel, MS

Lost in Thought

I breathe in the wind
you blow. The sun that hits my cheeks.
The clouds that pile up and make rain that taste so sweet. I watched the
stars that shine up above. Searching for my true love. It was our first
dance. It was also romance.

Breanna Perez
Panorama City, CA

When You Look Inside a Girl

When you look inside a girl
You see how much she really cries
When you look inside a girl
You see how much she really lies
When you look inside a girl
You see how much she can really love
When you look inside a girl
You can see how much she really hates you
When you look inside a girl
You can see how much she really is hurting
When you look inside a girl
You see how much she really sees you
When you look inside a girl
You see how you never know what to expect!

Diamond Kindel
Louisville, KY

382

My Little Sleepyhead

I wonder where you are
Is it somewhere far
In a land of make believe
That adults can't conceive
Sleepyhead.

Are you the king
Who had a magic ring
In a castle high
Reaching to the sky
Sleepyhead

Or are you in a magic town
With candy all around
Chocolate covered lanes
And lighted candy canes
Sleepyhead.

Maybe you're in outer space
Searching for a different race
Headed for the stars
Or maybe even Mars
Sleepyhead.

Well, wherever you may be
Will you please take me
To your land without a care
Will you take me there
My little sleepyhead.

Faye Lichbach
Silver Spring, MD

Listen to My Heart

I stand in a place that's dark and very cold, the tears are streaming down my face, no one seems to understand how I feel, if only you would listen to my heart.

I've been running oh for so long and trying to survive is getting harder each day, down on bended knees I pray, will someone please listen to my heart.

Broken inside my feelings I cannot hide, unreachable, untouchable, unlovable, is what man perceives of me, you can know who I am by listening to my heart.

Loneliness I have truly experienced, disappointment I've had my share, saying within myself I cannot bear these burdens alone, I need someone to listen to my heart.

I've come to the middle of the road, not knowing where it will take me, I believe there's something better in store for me, and it is when I listen to my heart

Dianne Johnson
Lebanon, KY

Thomas Chatterton

Possessed of impetuous charm
Tempered by youth's hasty stride,
You carried from Bristol to Brooke Street
A swift event-filled pride.

In less than one-half year,
Caught between madness and despair,
You forsook life for radiant dread
Leaving an enticing trace of genius
Disproportionate to your time.

Friends proclaimed your countenance fair,
Yet imagination must assist to restore
For no likeness was conserved.
Though your impulsive death lies in distant past,
The core of your poetic strike harbors
Raw controversy enough to last.

Ron Matros
Mesilla, NM

Some Day I Will Be Loved

I once loved a girl in the years of my youth.
With eyes like the summer, full of beauty and truth.
Early one morning, I found out she had fled.
She left me a note and here's what it said:
Someday you will be loved.
Feeling so low and wanting to be dead
As the deep red blood ran down the needle and thread
Not knowing how the story would end
Because each broken heart will eventually mend
Someday I will be loved. I will be loved.
I will be loved. Like I have never known
The memories of her will seem like bad dreams.
Just a series of blurs like they never occurred.
Someday I will be loved
Though I may feel alone as I'm falling asleep
Feeling each tear as it falls down my cheek.
I know my heart belongs to you
Someone I've just met so fresh and so new
Someday we will be loved
We will be loved.
We will be loved.
Today we are loved.

Nigel Clarke
Santa Barbara, CA

My name is Nigel A. Clarke. I was born in a town called Dustable in England. I'm the former British and USA ballroom dancing champion, and I've been competing for 33 years. This is the first poem I have ever written. Last year the fabulous woman I had spent the last 10 years with decided our relationship was over. I spent 6 months trying to find myself and along the way found a woman who changed my life and gave me back my confidence as a man. This poem is about the raw emotions I was going through and how out of something dying comes rebirth.

Fantasy Land

Dragons and lollypops and little boys too, are part of a fantasy of a world that is so true.

A boy named Michael John and his grandpa too, are riding the range and fighten Bandits and Sioux.

They camp in the hills next to a fire so bright; their blanket rolls are damp from forging rivers so wide.

They're off in a dream where there's cabins to build and treasure of gold waiting for them in the hills.

Now Michael's a sapling as straight as a post, with muscles like oxen and skin brown as toast.

He could take on Griz with only his hands and pa would just laugh and say, dumb bear you can't win!

We have many miles to travel this day, in this fantasy land. I wish we could stay.

We will float those rivers and climb those hills, bring down an elk and maybe some quail.

We'll live off the land and thank God for the right, and remember him in our prayers at night.

This journey I fear is coming near its end, for I hear the birds chirping, the dawn is at hand.

Now stick close to grandpa ya hear Michael John, for there'll be plenty more of those midnights to dawn.

Leo A. Heiney
Loveland, CO

Being the youngest of thirteen children and a very inspiring mother, I started writing verse as a very young boy. When my grandson was born, he was the first of six. I have written a poem for each of them when they were born. "Fantasy Land" was inspired by my three sons who went fishing and hunting with me but were always out-fished by their sister.

Been on This Road Before

I've seen things I was too blind to see
Felt things I was too numb to feel
Couldn't pass certain points in
My life but, I refuse to fail
Couldn't travel on water but somehow
I was able to sail
Ain't I been on this road before
Tragic re-runs of my life keep
getting shown
The same cycle continues to come and go
I've been on this path and my
Conscience knows
I shouldn't travel back on this road
So what keeps giving me the
Power to move on
If I've been on this road before

John M. Townsend
Texarkana, TX

Ode to a Daffodil

Oh, daffodil, oh daffodil,
you doth thy heart so good,
thy sweet daffodil.
Your delightful spring flower,
I dearly devour.
Oh, daffodil, oh daffodil,
Stay with thee,
Live on for another day.
Please live
for thy lonely heart
may rejoice in your delicate bloom.
Your golden trumpet
plays for thee.

William F. Koji
Canterbury, CT

My Teeth Are Turning Black

I never brush my teeth so my teeth are turning black
There's a cavity on every one
And they are growing mold and plaque
I think I need braces and a retainer too
A mouth brace would be miserable for everything I do
But the worst thing of all that is happening to my teeth
Is they are being checked by a dentist
Right as I speak.

Olivia R. Giddings
Milwaukee, WI

Tunnel in Our Eyes

I catch a quick glance, a look in your eyes
And the inaudible screams and whispers, they all disappear for that one moment
It's quick, barely noticeable, but I try to elongate your presence in my mind
And I remember each flash of quiet
Your eyes are a window, your lips are a door
One is closed, the other is open
But it leaves so much a mystery, so much I want to see inside
I've broken things, in other houses
The shattered glass I walked across, the scars to prove it
But I have never given up on you
I have learned, I have grown, I am ready to come inside
But the draft is bitter cold, the lock is jammed, the key is stuck
It keeps me at a distance
But I see a glimmer sometimes, a star in the sky that is my own
It seems to rest and reflect at your window
A tunnel in our eyes, something only we see
And just for that instant, we break away, into the warmth of your home
I memorize your smooth motions
Your subtle nuances, your brow, your hands, your lips
Your silhouette, your angles, your laugh, your light, the epitome of what I dream
The fronts and currents may push us away now, but someday your heart will open to me
Your door will creak and you will invite me inside through the tunnel in our eyes

Frankie Sparks
Hicksville, NY

Horriffying Cries

I heard a scream for help
On that dark and gloomy night.
I ran out the door
With nothing but fright.
When I saw what I saw
Lying on the ground,
I turned around and called
911 with a disturbing sound.
People came over with horror of cries
Holding and hugging each other till it all dies.
We had prayed hour after hour
For it to be a dream
But all we heard from each other
Was a wake of a scream.
Tossing and turning all through the night
Wondering why?
I didn't even get to say those
Last words of cry.
I love you, Mom,
Until the day I die.

Virginia Vogt
Chicago, IL

When Your Heart Turns Cold

When your heart turns cold
It causes your soul to freeze
It spreads throughout your spirit
Like a ruthless feeling disease
The walls that was once down
Now stand firm and tall
Safe from hate/love, pain/joy
Until you feel nothing at all
When your heart turns cold
A baby's cry means nothing
A dead corpse is trivial
Mothers neglecting children daily
Loneliness becomes your routine friend
Death seems like tranquility
Sleeping is never pleasant
If you even sleep at all
You forget ideals and turn off the reason
To make sure the product gets sold
You do not understand how I behave
Just wait till your heart turns cold.

Donald Modicue
Monroe, LA

Do You Know Me?

Smile and stay positive is what I must do
Another long day soon will be through
Conversations are limited…the main love is food
I'm walking on egg shells to avoid change in mood
Explain and repeat always trying to please
I have to remember…it's just the disease
Times of temper and anger increase as do fears
The hurt runs so deep and we both shed our tears
This cruel hurtful breast crawls into the brains
Then takes charge and devours 'til all intellect drains
Though our doors are unlocked…I'm still in a cage
A support group may help, but is it worth risking rage?
Lonely and alone…social options have grown few
Where can we go? Who can we laugh with or what can we do?
Soon this terrible villain, as our researchers claim
Will be harnessed and dealt with…Alzheimer's the name.

Joanne Rademacher
Daytona Beach, FL

We Are One

Help me;
Be my friend;
I am alone—
Or are the hordes of times past with me?

Do they walk where I walk,
Feel what I feel;
And will also those who are yet to come?

Yes, they are with me,
And I with them.
We are one.

I will help them;
I will be their friend;
They will never be alone.
All of us together forever;
Humanity.

Louzanna Marcum
Ewing, VA

Reflecting

As the cold settles in on a late winter's day
I look out my window, my mind far away.

I think of my youth and what might could have been
If only I'd listened to things I heard then.

The talks about schooling, a four-year degree,
My teacher said this was the pathway for me.

But love's more important, especially in youth
And 40 years later, I now have the proof.

My lifetime partner, the love of my life,
Way back then did make me his wife.

There's been love and support and children as well;
What more could I want? I just couldn't tell.

For these are the things God gifted to me
And knew I'd be happy and as fulfilled as could be.

Filomena E. Shepperson
Petersburg, VA

Present Darkness

City sidewalks lined with cracks
Walking slow as cars pass by
Carry burdens on our backs
Drop them now so you can fly

High above the streets and lights
Catch a glimpse of mystery
Spending all these city nights
Wishing we were truly free

Oh civilized society
Where not a soul can plainly see
The truth behind the mystery
Which lies within our history

Society's reality revealed
By true divinity
Above the clouds the stars shine bright
Through present darkness shines their light

Devin Hitchcock
Middle Point, OH

Prayer—What Does Prayer Mean to Me?

Prayer to me is the very start
It's me and him together, it's me talking to God, heart to heart.
A key
That opens my heart to him, just like his heart is always open to me.
Prayer to me is so very sweet,
It's also, like, a two-way street.
It's praising God, Listening to God, Learning about God.
It's Love + Beauty,
It's God opening my eyes to see, whatever it is, he wants me to see.
Never having to feel alone,
Like a feeling of comfort, relaxing, like feeling at home.
Prayer to me, is God and me.
Like a very Best Friend,
It's me and God together, to the very end.
Prayer is for everyone too,
Something personal, the Bottom Line – prayer is God and you.

Hope Hillyer
Middletown, IA

Three

The spot is empty now.
A hole exists where life once flourished,
Where love flowed like molten lava,
Capturing everyone in its path.
That little corner of the room was his.
Where he realized the power he had,
Even over the most unhappy soul.
I see memories floating in that corner now,
Like spirits being twirled around by a light breeze.
All melting into one.
He knew my deepest secrets,
My innermost thoughts.
I would talk to him everyday.
He saw me laugh and cry,
At my best and my worst,
And never judged me.
He trusted me, and I betrayed that trust.
He went with me willingly, without question.
Not knowing what was to come.
Today I put my dog to sleep,
To spare him pain and suffering,
But who will spare mine?
He's been but gone an hour,
And already I miss him deeply.

Denise English
Fords, NJ

Home

All my true life I had a home
With a bed fit for a mean queen or king
Furniture to live and die for
A table that could seat sixty, well six
A bathroom so full of reality and serenity
A hallway like the Holland tunnel
Six big blinking windows filled with souls
That fire escape shaped like a ship took me
Within, below, above and beyond it all
But as of Feb. 7, 08
I no longer have a home to call my own
My bed is no longer mine
My furniture has been taken away
My table I left standing all alone
My bathroom is a good old memory
That tunnel is a hallway to nowhere now
Those six windows are great big empty holes
And that fire escape is just another way out
Another outcast am I, left to wonder
And roam until I can find another
Place to call home

Angela Ellis
Brooklyn, NY

Ode to a B

Oh me… a B.
Not an A, but better than a C.
Is it better to be a B or not to be a B?
To never see whether you're an A or a D?
Not to know what you've achieved?
Or to accept being a B and to be doubt-free…
Or could it be better to be some other letter…entirely?
Like S, R, Q, or Z…
It is easy, you see, to be a B.
But how would it be to be L, M, N, O, or P?
How would it be to be running free as an S as in "sea," U as in
"umbrella,"
Or T as in "tree?"
Would it not be more good to be understood as a letter other than B…
Such as H as in "hood?"

—not precisely—

To be a B
Is to completely
Be what you were meant to be
Despite scrutiny
From A, D, F, and C…
So maybe
It is more noble and free
To stand as a B
Than as some other falsity.

Ida R. Wellborn
Gatlinburg, TN

Your Baby Brother

The day I brought home your baby brother,
you didn't know what to think of your Mother.
It took you a while to figure out,
What a baby brother was all about.
But, you got used to him, and it didn't take long,
you'd play with him, then sing him a song.
He became like a big doll to you.
Mom and Dad got a hug every now and then, too.
At that time you couldn't exactly know,
how close together you and he would grow.
What brother wanted, you'd see he had,
and he loved every bit of it, that little lad!
To be happy, you'll need each other's tender love,
just like the flowers need the rain from above.
Today, and always, you'll have need for each other,
'cause you're his only sis, and he's your only brother.
There will be times when you won't agree,
That's just brother and sister nature, you see.
But once the disagreement is all said and done,
You'll be closer than ever, having even more fun.
I love you both from the bottom of my heart.
You've made my life happy, right from your very start.
With love we'll face life-both the bad and the good.
Just having you two to love, is the joy of motherhood.

Judy C. Ratcliff
Chilhowie, VA

The Ideal Job

Is something you like to do?
Doing it at home and getting
pay for it.
You can walk around in your
pj's and work.
And when it rains or snows,
You can look out your window.
Look at the gas you can save.
Miss that lousy traffic.
Can you see that ideal job?

Janet Epps
Romulus, MI

Ode to the Porch

You are the reason I love this home
My summer Soltice; May party source
I yearn for you each winter
I stand gazing through the glass
    Door and picture your Summer glory
March signals your arrival—though premature
Soon we will toast your official debut with
    flowering baskets, candles, a fountain,
    and, of course, rocking chairs
Many lust for you, The Porch—My Porch
I will never let you go.

Gale Schiefferle
Dublin, OH

Moonlight

A herd would tire
As they travel by moonlight
A quiet shadow in the night
Leaving delicate prints in the snow

They are rarely seen alone
Instead they travel together
Running as one
They talk by moonlight
Singing their age-old songs
The cold does not matter
For they fear nothing

Through wind, rain, snow, and ice
They will survive
Living the same way their ancestors did
Not so long ago

Kim Moore
Effingham, SC

Thanksgiving Leaves

Fall leaves are like Thanksgiving dinner;
yellow like squash, red like cranberry sauce,
orange like pumpkin pie, and brown like the
turkey roasting in the oven, in the breeze
through the eyes of me.

Susan M. Chance
Hampton, GA

Autumns spent in Maine was the inspiration to the writing of "Thanksgiving Leaves."
now reside in Hampton, Georgia with my spouse and five-year-old daughter. I recently
completed a two-year course in Children's Literature through the Institute of Children'
Literature, May 24, 2008. I continue to be inspired by the beauty and wonder of God'
creation, which leads me to primarily write poetry based on nature that surrounds m
environment.

Christmas Eve Remembered

My path of footprints filled with snow
Which sparkled from street lamp's soft glow.
One long deep breath of winter's air
Helped push away a teenage care.

White towered church in my town's square
And organ music drew me there.
Four stained glass windows filtered light
Shed a welcome that special night.

We sang of Christ's birth of long ago
As church pews filled with candles glow.
The wooden pews were unvarnished and worn.
I thought of the stable where Christ was born.

The sweet smell of hay in His manger bed
Would have wafted around Christ's cushioned head.
As Mary smiled down upon her haloed boy
She knew God's gift of love would bring great joy.

God's light sent to us through Jesus' birth
Is mankind's beacon to peace on earth.
On Christmas Eve as we sing "Holy Night"
We thank God for His gift of love and light.

As Christmas Eve bells ring 'round the earth
The bells remind us of Christ's holy birth.
We recall the message of the midnight bells
To let God's love in and serve Him well.

Dorothy Jenkins Shorts
Milwaukee, WI

Script

Write me out of perfect misery, into oblivious, unknown content.
Write me anywhere. A million miles away or
deep at the bottom of your love.
Read me into the heartbeat of the world;
hard as stone, yet smooth and worn.
Write me unglued in the place I am stuck,
pressing into myself a rock of hurt, small and uneventful.
See me. A thousand times over. Ever the same ways.
Move me forward and show me how to leave behind.
Write me into perfection.
Dream for me that which I can't for myself.
Read me life and loss so true that it numbs me to feel.
Skip a beat because I mean everything.
Face yourself in me, underneath the highest cloud.
Miss me through eternity and after.
Steal the secrets that I hide inside tears that come from tired eyes.
Write me out and in again. But pick up in a different place this time.
Read me more alive than now because all I really need is then.
Break me, breathe me, better than before.
Write me a life so simple it shatters.
Say that it is everything it should be.
Among ways that force you to wait, stay with me. However possible.
Stay in places that I know that I can see clearly so they don't ever fade
Write me where you are. Say it all over again.

Ashley Churchill
Bristol, CT

The Antique Shop

A little shack by the shore
Sells many treasures, antiques galore.

Teakettles tarnished with ripe age,
Books, thin paged, edges frayed,
Crystal glasses, pot and pans,
Bottles filled with shells and sand,
Vintage clothes and jeweled pins,
Photo-overflowing bins,
Slightly yellow, tiny pearls,
Porcelain dolls of pretty girls,
Old-fashioned shoes and lots of lace,
Eyeglasses in a rough leather case.

See the sign that says 'Open' on the door,
Leads to all of these and many more,
At that antique shop on the beaten shore.
These treasures are no longer used,
And so are taken somewhere new,
To receive another chance at life,
And the life lies with you.

Though this generation is young, and we have a long way to go,
There will come a day when we all will grow old,
And in the end we all will loan,
Many antiques of our own.

Stephanie A. Dell'Aira
Hicksville, NY

Great Sand Dunes of Colorado

Sand shifts in the breeze.
Curving waves are on the dunes.
A grain trickles down.

Nancy E. Harris
Greeley, CO

Corporate Country

On whose shoulder rests the burden of life,
The land or the Lord?
Who control whom, in this perilous strife,
Who here wields the sword?

A blade that may take, may also be just
And its master most merciful too
Ending life with just one thrust,
If that is their aim to do

With country the Land, and corporation the Lord,
Who defends people between?
By whose hand is held, the almighty sword,
In this daily unfolding scene?

Rebecca Benison
Valley Stream, NY

Bright, Shining Eyes

As the "eighties" ended, her life began,
This daughter of our daughter became part of our clan.
Her enormous, dark eyes always shining so bright,
Made all of our lives seem ever so right.
Everyone who met her was drawn to those eyes,
So intelligent, so magnetic, so sweet, and oh so wise.
All animals she held in such high esteem,
And they returned this affection, or so it seemed
Most favored were her horses, and accomplished she became,
All her many equine endeavors brought so much fame.
At 17 she intended to became an animal's vet,
But instead one day she came to us all, quite upset.
A mistake had been made- a baby's life was a stake,
But to end this child's life was not a decision she would make.
Just out if high school was the 18 year old boy,
Together they decided this news would become joy.
As her HS junior year ended, their marriage vows were said,
They had just two months to prepare a home and baby's bed.
Then all of our prayers for a healthy baby God heard,
He would not give more than she could handle, true to his word.
We discovered an 18 year old girl could be a wonderful mom,
All while graduating with honors and attending her prom; with those
bright eyes still shining.
P.S. In case you're wondering, she's a college student now,
But her favorite time is as a wife and mother; and of her we are so proud.

Sandy Barrett
Lincoln, AR

409

Your Word (John 21:25)

On your word I shall rely
until the day I earthly die.
Nothing less satisfies
nothing else is worth the time!
Superior wisdom is found within:
for those believing; earthly well-being.
Perfectionism is it story
and only thru Jesus will you see its glory:
The words, The sentences,
The paragraphs, The chapters,
The books; The old confirmed by the new.
All literally alive and living
from a Father lovingly giving.
Oh' it's total understanding
we will one day grasp
when the Righteous One
comes at last!

Ralph C. Forrest
Winfield, IL

Skeptic Mind in Love

Growing up, hubris wars,
Me-them friends and foes:
Blood, sweat, tears are your
Until reaching my toes

Surprise, they are mine.
Survive, no high walls;
Pause, share a glass of wine…
More games with cotton balls

I miss the God I fake,
From mock versions to Awe IT,
Evolved framing, what I make,
Shared divinity doesn't fit

Existence. Our formulations
In submission or defiance,
Are fond guesses, fictions, delusions…
Key stones for truth in balance
SUPREME IT acts through chance
Reverence, part of the action.
Presence in living, what a stance…
A skeptic mind satisfaction.

Jose Sousa
Swansea, MA

My name is Jose Sousa. I was born in the Azores, Portugal, where I graduated in medicine.
I recently retired from my professional practice in psychiatry. Now I have time to read
more and tend a homestead named "Back to Nature." My children have called me a
"Catholic atheist." I take this as being positively skeptical and also humanistic. My wife,
Olivia, prays and goes to church while I read science and tend the farm. Although I never
developed a need to emulate an uncle who published poetry, I wrote this poem when
retired to describe who I am.

In the Back of My Mind

There has been many men
in my life
no one will ever really know of
them except me
But two of them are my
Brothers and they will
always be.

Cindy Geary
Grass Range, MT

We are Meant to be

As I look into your brown eyes,
my stomach begins to get butterflies.
The pain and loneliness goes away,
happiness is no longer a stray.
It starts to rush through my heart,
hoping that we never, ever part.
It's a feeling I have never felt before, you are like an adventure; a closed
door.
Waiting to be opened by your soul mate,
picking the door that you were behind
was our fate.

Ciara Romero
Rockaway Park, NY

Untitled

Tell me something good amidst the 2008 appalling news
Just everyone in the media has his opinions and views
I am sick to death of hearing of political corruption & abuse
Why can't the media bring forth pieces that will amuse?
I want to hear something good about America not what we lose.

Where's the hope we citizens are yearning to see once more?
Can we all come together and realize our country is poor
And that we need to heal, from the top on down,
We need new blood in the White House, we can't fool around
Let's hope Barack Obama and Congress will open a new door.

Stop the fighting amongst union and management we cry
We want to see more bipartisan in the works gone so awry
Bring on the levelheaded, the common sense intelligence we need
Most Americans work hard for we have loving families to feed
We long to see our grassroots kept alive, please don't let that die.

Where is that country we once treasured so well?
Where honesty reigned and our courts upheld the swell,
You know that land of the free where responsibility ranked high
And all citizens could enjoy a big piece of the pie
Has corruption tainted the very meaning of our Liberty Bell?

May God protect our beautiful Statue of Liberty from harm,
For she stands on our New York Harbor and will forever sound an alarm
Her gesture salutes our troops who protect our great land
Don't forget this great lady and the torch in her hand
She stands for freedom and truth, that is her charm!!

Toni Twiggs
Ft. Myers, FL

He's the Reason for the Season

This is a story of the greatest of Love
Sent down to us from almighty God up above
For God so loved His children on this planet called earth
He showed us according to Him what we're truly worth

Because we all fall short of His goal
And could not pay the debt that we owe
So God sent to us His perfect son
To pay for the sins of everyone

In the age of being politically correct
Each and every store I'll be careful to select
If all that they can say is Happy Holiday
None of my business will be going their way

In God we trust is still on our coin
His loving army I'm proud to join
Therefore this is why I cannot deny
If they can't put Merry Christmas on their sign
Into that business I will have to decline

He's the reason for this season
So I say Merry Christmas to you
Black or White, Muslim, Gentile or Jew

Charles Edwards
Indainapolis, IN

Sweet Changes

A world overturned in beige.
The grasses, like humans, age.
All, white and black without night.
The stars shall come soon—twilight
Be the only thing alive,
And life asleep deep inside.

A rainbow of hues living on green.
The pale morning frost, in light, does gleam.
Far too beautiful to explain;
Words too lame to use in this way.
The bite of the wind scorns with chill.
Banished by light, not by its will.

An ocean of blue flows above so high
And gray then swallows it and starts to cry.
The storm is swift and frightening,
With rain and thunder and lightning.
But soon it comes to pass and so
The ocean's white goes to and fro.

Flames engulf the forest's leaf.
Autumn sword so quick unsheathed.
The once curious fauna hides in it wait
For cold to come early and leave so late.
Flora was once bright and bold,
Now human with age dies old.

Madeline Marmon
Little Falls, MN

A Farmer's Heaven

I'm sure there's a place in Heaven,
Where John Deere and Farmall both run.
Where those who farmed upon the earth
Can go to have some fun.

The Father is a wise God.
The Lord knows a farmer's heart.
A farmer needs to turn the sod
And I know He'll do His part.

A part of Heaven is set aside
For farmers, He's called above.
And there with tractors they'll abide,
A way God shows His love.

There's every implement they need
To work they're bit of land.
There's also every kind of seed,
Given by the Master's hand.

So farmer, Please do not despair
When it comes your time to go.
I'm sure there's tractors there,
Just like the one you loved below.

Connie C. Kingsolver
Jamestown, OH

My Fight Within

I'm abnormal, that's my case.
Tragedy and heartache are the small things I've faced.
Scattered in pieces I've sat alone,
in my dark bedroom corner at home.
Patiently waiting for the pain to go away,
disappointment is the price I unwillingly pay.
Tears fall endlessly torturing my mind,
wondering if I'm the only "one of a kind."
Numb, broken and tortured inside,
nothing left but courage and pride.
Fighting for strength I hopelessly stood.
Winning my fight, I knew I could.
Scared and afraid I bravely stand tall.
Courageously refusing never to fall.
Scars reopened like a flood of crushed dreams.
It's all up to me, no support from a team.
I cried tears of hurt unknown to mankind,
My fate and destiny I'm unable to find.
Staggering and tired I pick up my feet,
fighting back to the rhythm of my own beat.
Painlessly numb I've won my war,
Through the sky with a smile I soar.
Content and happy, I've faced the dark,
A unforgettable memory has now left its mark.
My fears overcome, my fight laid to sleep,
My mirror reveals my enemy, and the secret I keep.

Shaaron Townsend
Pickens, SC

The Story

Tears falling from my eyes
Black running down my cheek.
You would think someone dies,
But the ending you must seek.

This is the beginning
Not even close to the end.
My story writes itself
With the help of a ballpoint pen.

You walk in the door with flowers
And drop them by my feet.
Now you must count the hours
Before my heart will skip a beat.

You look deep into my eyes
Until you reach my soul.
Then I start the cries,
Which you thought began to dull.

The end is almost near, I say.
Our time is pretty much done.
But we have until the end of the day.
Good night...My sweet... LOVE.

Trisha Gallagher
West Chester, PA

No Matter What

John is my son's name
And no matter wherever you are
You will always be near
No matter how far
Because I love you
You will always be near
Because that is the way I'll feel no matter what!

Loretta Maurer
Durham, NC

Little Ones

Hold them when their feeling bad.
Hug them when their feeling sad.
Kiss them on their cheeks so bright.
Tuck them safely in at night.
Give them full time not your spare.
Show them that you really care.
They'll warm your heart in a special way.
While you watch them as they play.
Listen with your heart and mind.
As they grow you will find.
These little ones from above.
Will return your kindness with their love.

George H. Steinacker
Salisbury, MD

Differences

No two people are the same.
Even though some share a name.
We all are our own person inside.
Sometimes we may feel the need to hide.
When you see someone that looks different than you.
Don't be so quick to judge, try on their shoe.
We all must live and learn.
You better be careful or you may burn.
The people you think are different are really brave.
They are not scared to go for what they crave.
When you look down on others tastes.
What you're really doing is such a waste.
Don't spend all your time criticizing others.
Instead treat each other like brothers.
If you treat everyone kind.
That will give you peace of mind.

Melvin A. Rainey, Jr.
High Point, NC

Visions

Often I think about the days when I was a child,
and immediately my imagination starts running wild.
I remember the first tree house the other boys and I made;
While farther down the street the little girls sold ice-cold lemonade.
The school that I attended at the end of the block,
All of its windows are busted out now and the doors are padlocked.
When it used to be safe for the kids to go hangout in the park,
Just as long as we got back home before it was dark.
I wonder what ever happened to my old friends, the Jaworskys and the
Browns;
They are probably dead by now or else done moved to another town.
However I'll always have fond memories of this old neighborhood,
Tho' now there's only a vacant lot where our house once stood.
In fact most of these old homes are boarded up around here;
Although the City Council still talks about tearing them down every
year. Well recently some new folks came and moved in across the street;
although they're most likely drug dealers hoping they can hustle to make
ends meet.
And even tho' the police come and make arrests, and confiscates the
goods,
It only seems to encourage more bad folks to move in this old
neighborhood.
Because we know it's a fact that people are no longer safe in their own
home,
Especially the old and the convalescent who are now living alone.
Crime's done skyrocketed like a jet airplane,
And the economy is way down, due to the loss of jobs, but nobody wants
to accept the blame.
Maybe by the time I return a few changes will already be made around
this old place;
And if nothing more, at least I hope someone will be done cut the tall
grass around these abandoned houses.
Because its already grown up to my waist.

James Logan, Jr.
Detroit, MI

An Ode to Frye Island, Maine

My dad built my family a summer home in Maine
It caused him a lot of sleepiless nights and back pain
It is on Frye Island, to get there we take a ferry
When we get to our house, we can pick blueberries
The house is a log cabin on a dead-end street
There are lots of great people we always meet
To get to the beach, I go through the trail on my bike
But sometimes I will even walk, run, or hike
On Sebago Lake we always have fun
We swim to cool off from the hot summer sun
We all sit by the fire when it's late at night
We make smores, laugh and play tag with flashlights.
I always have fun in Maine in the summer
When it's over and school starts, it's always a bummer!

Jake Kelley
Dracut, MA

Before and After

Weather beaten moon beam eyes
They speak to me, it's no surprise.
Tender kiss upon my palm
More soothing than a gentle balm
From lips so furred and gray.

Angelic face did not betray
That pain was suffered in a day
Or week or month, or year.
Thin body tho revealed much more
And every blistered oozing sore
I felt as if my own

Then churning tides pulled you from me.
And pondering what could set you free
Wept out what there was to give.
But tears outpouring couldn't save you.
All the while the thought was
How brave you looked to passersby.

Then peace came, softly, without warning
Turned away and with that morning
You were gone.
Now restless winds go sweeping by
And in the blinking of an eye
I stop, and think of you.

Kim Costello
Branford, CT

In His Presence

On her final journey through the dark night,
She walked ever so softly into the light.
She beheld His face and kneeled down before Him
With angels around her, they all would adore Him.

He said to her—His voice calm and clear,
"Welcome to Heaven. I'm so glad you are here.
Your grace and compassion left me no doubt—
You're a special angel Heaven can't do without."

She was in His presence—what awe that inspired!
She didn't remember being sick and tired.
He sat on His throne—she at His feet—
She had longed for this day: her Savior to meet.

They talked for hours and walked streets of gold.
Angels smiled as they passed—both the young and the old;
But somehow up here they looked much the same.
No babies were crying—no one crippled or lame.

Peace and joy everywhere, beyond comprehension;
And this was not of her own mind's invention.
Rather, fulfillment of God's promise and love.
She's now in His presence—with the lamb and the dove.

Anna L. Aytes
Lakewood, CO

Success?

Perpetually I seem to wonder
If what I did should be put asunder
To deny my choice without a blunder
Leaves me fearfully staring at gifts

Sophia Pappageorge
Chicago, IL

Winter Wonderland Delight

An unexpected storm of rain and snow,
To a barren earth ascribed a frosty glow;
Fallen tree trunks were like icy sliding boards,
Frost was on the pumpkins, ice upon the gourds.
Meadows of grasses were carpeted white,
Fresh impressions of the seasonal delight.
Promontories bore snow queens of whit moss.
Slippery the path that we had to cross.
Fields of thistle and goldenrod tops.
Spent blossoms were transformed into cotton balls,
Popsicle cones hung from hemlock trees tall.
Frozen breath on cat's whiskers starkly white,
All in all, quite a scintillating sight.

Katharina M. Lauer
Stillwater, PA

Singles Mingle

What does it means to be single?
Does it means not to mingle
Because of being one, and not a couple?
This could be real trouble for some who make decisions
on the double.
Should I go alone and take a chance,
Or wait for that someone to be enhanced?
Now I know I am complete and true to me.
It's O.K. to be single,
As for me, I can and will mingle.
How Shall I mingle—with you in my mind—through my
thoughts?
Can it be with you and others touching of whom I have not
sought?
Oh! The distractions and interruptions are such invasions.
I think I will need lots or persuasion.
Why should I let go of my single status,
When love, in its purest form, is all that matters?
So come on singles-let us mingle!

Lataunya Wallace
Greenwood, MS

I'm Nobody's Mom

I sit and wait for the telephone to ring
or the doorbell to chime, or the postman
to bring a letter, But!
I'm nobody's Mom
Mother's Day comes, my birthday goes
by. Holidays come and go.
I am all alone.
I am nobody's Mom.

Helen Gollins
Deshler, OH

Darkness

Shattered faces,
Bewildered places,
Darkness lives in them.
Dim lights,
Lonely nights,
Darkness thrives on them.
A single ray of light will be smothered into dark,
While people slumber,
There they number,
And in the darkness lurk.

Abigail Volk
Vancouver, WA

I'm So Big

People come and People go.
Where they're going I do not know.
Snow is falling to the ground.
So many people all around.
I'm so big, yet feel so small.
No one notices me, no one at all.

I watch the street as cars go by.
No one stops, I wonder why.
A storm is coming, It's almost here.
Three feet of snow, that's what I fear.
I'm so big, yet I get I get so cold,
Never alone but have no one to hold.

I stand and wait for warmer days,
Picnics and parties and afternoon plays.
People will slow down and enjoy a walk,
They come to eat, read, or just talk.
I'm so big, yet no one can see,
How I how love being a tree.

Judy Melnick
Corydon, IN

Index of Poets

Y

Z

Printed in the United States
221082BV00001B/1/P